SCHUMANN

DICHTERLIEBE

An Authoritative Score

Historical Background · Essays in Analysis

Views and Comments

BACH CANTATA NO. 4
edited by Gerhard Herz

BACH CANTATA NO. 140
edited by Gerhard Herz

BEETHOVEN SYMPHONY NO. 5 IN C MINOR
edited by Elliot Forbes

BERLIOZ FANTASTIC SYMPHONY
edited by Edward T. Cone

BRAHMS VARIATIONS ON A THEME OF HAYDN, OPP. 56A AND 56B
edited by Donald M. McCorkle

CHOPIN PRELUDES, OPUS 28
edited by Thomas Higgins

DEBUSSY PRELUDE TO "THE AFTERNOON OF A FAUN"
edited by William W. Austin

HAYDN SYMPHONY NO. 103 IN E-FLAT MAJOR ("DRUM ROLL")
edited by Karl Geiringer

MOZART PIANO CONCERTO IN C MAJOR, K. 503
edited by Joseph Kerman

MOZART SYMPHONY IN G MINOR, K. 550
edited by Nathan Broder

PALESTRINA POPE MARCELLUS MASS
edited by Lewis Lockwood

SCHUBERT SYMPHONY IN B MINOR ("UNFINISHED")
edited by Martin Chusid

SCHUMANN DICHTERLIEBE
edited by Arthur Komar

STRAVINSKY PETRUSHKA
edited by Charles Hamm

Robert Schumann

DICHTERLIEBE

An Authoritative Score
Historical Background · Essays in Analysis
Views and Comments

Edited by
ARTHUR KOMAR

W · W · NORTON & COMPANY

New York · London

15082

Library of Congress Catalog Card No. 69-15708

ISBN 0 393 02147 5 Cloth Edition
ISBN 0 393 09904 0 Paper Edition

PRINTED IN THE UNITED STATES OF AMERICA

8 9 0

Contents

Preface

Robert Schumann's song cycle, *Dichterliebe*, is perhaps the best loved and most frequently performed cycle of lieder in the standard repertoire. The poems, by Heinrich Heine, are famous in their own right, both in the original German and in translation.

The initial section of this edition presents information about the collection of Heine's poems from which Schumann selected the texts of *Dichterliebe*. There is also biographical material about Schumann, and a non-technical description of the cycle—including details of the relation between the poems and the music. Also included are evaluations of Heine as a poet and of Schumann as an interpreter of Heine's poetry, as well as comparisons between *Dichterliebe* and some of Schumann's other well-known song cycles.

The score contained in this volume represents the first overall editorial revision of *Dichterliebe* to be published since Friedländer's work for Peters Edition more than sixty years ago. Although no new sources have materialized since then, careful examination of the original manuscript and the first edition reveals numerous discrepancies, particularly regarding details of phrasing, dynamics and tempo markings. Also included are four songs not generally known to have originally belonged to *Dichterliebe*, interpositioned according to the original order of the songs in the cycle. The purpose of including these additional songs is not to suggest that they be performed along with the other songs, but is merely to offer the reader a direct comparison between both versions of the cycle. English translations by Philip L. Miller are provided for all twenty songs.

The analysis section is divided into two parts. The first part consists of an extensive study of the coherence of the sixteen songs of

Dichterliebe as a totality. The material is aimed at the comparatively advanced student who wishes to consider this matter in depth. It is recommended that this essay be read in as close to one sitting as possible, lest the abundance of details obscure the continuity of the argument. The second part of the analysis section consists of five excerpted discussions and/or sketches of four of the individual songs (2–5) of *Dichterliebe*. Three of these contributions are by Heinrich Schenker, the Austrian theorist (1867–1935) whose influence is now being so strongly felt; the sketches of Song 3 are published here for the first time. The remaining contributions in this part are by two foremost Schenker authorities, Allen Forte and Felix Salzer. (The study of the complete cycle in the preceding part of the analysis section also makes use of Schenker's theories and analytic techniques.)

The final commentary section contains essentially non-technical material about Schumann as a song composer, a brief biographical study of Heine in his formative years as a poet, and numerous excerpts from letters and articles by Schumann on his and others' feelings and abilities as song composers.

ARTHUR KOMAR

HISTORICAL
BACKGROUND

From Heine's Poems into Schumann's Songs

In 1823, the twenty-five-year-old Heinrich Heine published the *Lyrisches Intermezzo*,[1] a collection of sixty-six short lyric poems, some of which had already appeared in literary journals. The poems soon achieved great popularity. Composers were quick to show an interest in Heine's poetry, and Schubert himself set six poems from the *Buch der Lieder* (Book of Songs) —a larger collection containing the *Lyrisches Intermezzo*, published in 1827—just before his death in 1828.

> Heine's *Buch der Lieder* has become a 'book of songs' in a sense other than that intended by its author. . . . [His] earlier poems have served the masters of the German Lied as a seemingly inexhaustible reservoir of texts. What attracted these composers to Heine is not difficult to see. His preference for simple strophic metres, his simple language and vivid though sparing imagery, whose import could reach an audience even when the words were sung, his terseness, which would prevent the song from going on too long, his penchant for suggesting certain attitudes and emotions without talking about them directly, which leaves scope for the piano accompaniment; and last but not least, the melodiousness of his language, that 'Singen und Klingen' of his words of which he himself was so proud—such things as these commended his poems to Schubert and Schumann, to Mendelssohn, Franz and Silcher, to Brahms, to Richard Strauss and to a host of other composers in Germany and abroad.[2]

Heine made numerous alterations in later editions of the *Lyrisches Intermezzo*, adding the present first poem (*Im wunderschönen Monat*

1. In a volume entitled *Tragödien nebst einem lyrischen Intermezzo*, containing two plays, with the poems inserted between them.
2. S. S. Prawer, *The Poet of the Buch der Lieder*, in *Heine, The Tragic Satirist*, Cambridge University Press, Cambridge, 1961, p. 1.

Mai), taking over *Ich grolle nicht* and two other poems from an earlier collection (*Minnelieder*, 1822), and deleting five other poems to make a final total of sixty-five poems. The final poem, published initially under the title *Sylvester-Abend*, had originally described the "old year so sad," rather than the "evil old songs," as it appears in the *Lyrisches Intermezzo*. The reference to the old year (1821) was apparently auto-biographical—Heine's cousin, Amalie, had reportedly rejected him in favor of another, whom she married in that year. In any case, the general mood of the *Lyrisches Intermezzo* is one of unrequited love—sometimes nostalgic, otherwise bitter.[3]

Heine's poetry had lost none of its popularity by 1840, the year in which Schumann relinquished his former distaste for song-writing (cf. page 123 below) and composed nearly 150 songs. Schumann's choice of poems from the *Lyrisches Intermezzo* can hardly be equated with Heine's alleged personal situation when writing them, as the loyalty of Schumann's fiancée—the celebrated pianist, Clara Wieck—was not in doubt. However, if not unrequited love, then frustrated marriage plans dominated Schumann's personal life at that time, due to the legally binding objections of Clara's father. In 1839, the young couple instigated a formal suit to win permission to marry, and all of Schumann's most famous song-cycles—including the two sets based on poems of Heine—were composed in the anxious months prior to the eventual favorable court ruling in August, 1840. (The marriage took place the following month.)

In its original form, the second and larger of these Heine cycles was called *Gedichte von Heinrich Heine, 20 Lieder und Gesänge aus dem lyrischen Intermezzo*. The songs were begun on May 24 and completed a week later. Prior to the first edition, published by Peters (Leipzig, 1844), four of the songs were removed, the dedication was changed (from Mendelssohn to the soprano Wilhelmine Schröder-Devrient[4]), and the title *Dichterliebe*[5] (literally, Poet's Love) was added.

3. For a critical examination of the relation between Heine's personal life and the poems of the *Lyrisches Intermezzo*, see William Rose, *The Early Love Poetry of Heinrich Heine, an Inquiry into Poetic Inspiration*, Oxford, 1962.

4. Schröder-Devrient was a much admired opera and lieder singer in Schumann's day. Wagner praised her highly, and she sang major soprano roles in first perform-ances of some of his operas. In a review of a concert that occurred on March 18, 1841, Schumann described her as "an artist and poetess who will always delight." Grieg thought well of her, too (cf. page 120, below). Schumann dedicated his three string quartets, Op. 41, to Mendelssohn; they appeared in print in 1843, a year before the first edition of *Dichterliebe*.

5. That Schumann acquiesced in the new title—if he did not actually choose it himself—would seem to be indicated by a letter to C. F. Peters, dated August 8, 1844, in which Schumann refers to the work by that name. Cf. F. Gustav Jansen, ed., *Robert Schumanns Briefe, Neue Folge*, 2nd ed., Leipzig, 1904, letter no. 518.

Since there is no actual narrative in the *Lyrisches Intermezzo*, Schumann's setting of just a portion of the collection presents no serious problem, especially as he retained the outer poems of the collection—proceeding from the happy beginning as love arises to the unhappy ending as love is buried. The following table shows the numerical placement of the twenty songs in relation to Heine's collection.[6] The principal images that intertwine throughout the lyrics of *Dichterliebe* are love, songs, flowers, dreams and tears. In all but the last of the final four songs, dreams are followed by disappointing awakenings, while in the last song the poet decides to bury all the dreams along with his songs.

Numerical Ordering of the Poems of Dichterliebe

In the composer's manuscript	In the first edition	In Lyrisches Intermezzo
1	1	1
2	2	2
3	3	3
4	4	4
5		5
6		6
7	5	7
8	6	11
9	7	18
10	8	22
11	9	20
12	10	40
13	11	39
14	12	45
15		46
16		54
17	13	55
18	14	56
19	15	43
20	16	65

Certain poems in the *Lyrisches Intermezzo* are linked to others by virtue of word repetitions: e.g. the first line of No. 18 ("Ich grolle nicht, und wenn das Herz auch bricht") is tied directly to the opening line of No. 19 ("Ja, du bist elend, und ich grolle nicht").[7] Only the

6. Schumann set one other poem from *Lyrisches Intermezzo*—No. 10, *Die Lotusblume*—a few months before composing *Dichterliebe*. This song was published as No. 7 in *Myrthen*, Opus 25.

7. Cf. Chapter 9, *The Skillful Arranger* in S. S. Prawer, *Heine: Buch der Lieder*, New York, 1962, p. 46 ff.

first of these two poems is found in *Dichterliebe*.[8] On the other hand, there is no lack of verbal associations among the sixteen poems remaining in *Dichterliebe*[9]: e.g. references to the Rhine River and the Cathedral at Cologne, in Songs 6 and 16, and the correspondence between Song 4, line 3 ("Doch wenn ich küsse deinem Mund") and Song 5, line 6 ("Wie der Kuss von ihrem Mund"). More important, the correspondence between the words "weinen bitterlich" in Song 4, line 8, and "weinte . . . bitterlich" in Song 13, lines 7-8, is underscored by a musical correspondence (cf. p. 89 below).

With one exception, all of the lyrics of *Dichterliebe* contain from two to eight 4-line verses; the exception, Song 3, contains just a single 6-line verse, but Schumann extended it to nearly eight lines by repeating from lines 3 and 4 at the end. The consistent use of 4-line verses is reflected in musical phrases of two, four, and eight bars (the most notable exception being the eleven-bar groupings of Song 14, containing a single 3/4 bar within an otherwise 2/4 context), but, of course, this is the norm for tonal music in any case. The generally square phrasing of the verses proper is offset by the wide variety of dimension in the piano postludes; *Dichterliebe* is justly famous for the fact that each of nine postludes (in Songs 5, 6, 8, 9, 10, 11, 12, 15, and 16) approximately equals or exceeds the length of the individual verses that precede it.

The verses exhibit three different rhyme schemes: *aabb*, *abab*, and *abcb*. However, there is nothing in the music that directly corresponds to these schemes. For example, in Song 2, an example of *abcb*, the same music is heard in verse 1 for lines 3 and 4 (*c, b*) as for lines 1 and 2 (*a, b*). Moreover, in verse 2, despite the presence of this same rhyme scheme, a new musical idea is introduced for the first two lines, followed in the last two lines by a varied recapitulation of the music of the first verse.

Schumann generally preserved the poems without excessive word repetitions or alterations, the principal exception being in *Ich grolle nicht* (cf. pp. 117-18 below). Moreover, there are few melismas—the singing of one syllable with two or more pitches—and the few that are found are very brief. The eight verses of Song 15 are taken from the original version of the poem, *Aus alten Märchen*, which Heine subse-

8. But Schumann compensated for this omission by adding the words "ich grolle nicht" to the *second* verse of No. 18. Cf. pp. 117-18 below, for a discussion of Schumann's revision of this poem.

9. Since I am mainly interested in describing Schumann's cycle in its final form, all further references to *Dichterliebe* omit Songs 4a, 4b, 12a, and 12b from consideration.

quently reduced to six verses in the 1844 edition of *Buch der Lieder*.

Only two of the songs (1 and 9) are musically strophic (i.e. all verses are set to the same music) and they each contain just two verses. (By comparison, eight of the twenty songs of Schubert's *Die schöne Müllerin* are strophic, and six of them contain from three to five verses.) In *Dichterliebe*, even the two strophic songs are not entirely repetitive: in Song 1, the piano interlude following verse 1 differs slightly—but not insignificantly—from both the introduction to the first verse and the postlude after the second verse; and Song 9 treats each verse-half as a musical section, the second section differing from the first, so that the strophic effect is minimized. Six other songs are semi-strophic: Songs 5, 7, and 12 each contain two verses, the second of which digresses at some point after the similar beginning; and Songs 8, 13, and 14 each contain more than two verses, with only the final one differing from the first. There is nothing about the individual poems to indicate which songs are musically strophic. Thus, while verses 1 and 2 of Song 1 scan alike—implying strophic treatment of the vocal part of the song—verses 1 and 2 of Song 4 also scan alike, yet this song is "through-composed" (i.e. it has no repetition of large musical sections). Furthermore, verses 1 and 2 of Song 8 do *not* scan alike, yet are treated alike musically, with slight adjustments to accommodate the verbal differences (Ex. 1). Of the non-strophic songs, some contain a musical recapitulation following a contrasting middle section (Songs 2, 15, and 16), while the remaining "through-composed" songs contain recapitulatory material in their postludes—with the exception of Song 4, in which literal repetition plays virtually no role whatsoever.

Ex. 1 Comparison of verses 1 and 2, Song 8

The popular success of Heine's early poetry was followed eventually by critical rejection in this country,[10] but in recent years Heine has been regaining some of his earlier prestige. Certainly, of all the German poets represented among Schumann's songs, Heine has fared as well as any of the others, with the obvious exception of Goethe. I personally prefer the Eichendorff poems of Schumann's *Liederkreis*, Op. 39, to the Heine poems of *Dichterliebe*. There is nothing in *Dichterliebe* as good as the text of *Mondnacht*, nor anything in Op. 39 as bad as *Allnächtlich im Traume* (Song 14 in *Dichterliebe*).[11]

In any event, the significance of the quality of the poem in a song is a controversial issue. Clearly, if you understand the language, you will prefer good poetry to bad. But one can think of countless examples where the music leaves the words far behind, and yet the song is good—whereas a good text can never counterbalance bad music. The main point is that one can appreciate the music of a song without understanding the words, while one can receive little idea of a song at all from

10. "Heine himself had few hopes of the success of his collection, and his usually so knowledgeable and wily publisher, Julius Campe, had been unwilling to bring the book out at all. Yet in the end it was on the *Buch der Lieder* more than on any other that the fortunes of the house of Campe were founded and that the poet's own fame was to rest. It was read and discussed at tea tables and evening parties; young ladies wept over it and businessmen sniggered at its jokes; empresses cherished it; statesmen (even when, like Friedrich von Gentz or Metternich himself, they were bitterly opposed to everything Heine stood for in politics) counted it among their favourite reading; composers found in it an inexhaustible source of texts for their songs; and scores of poets and poetasters paid it the compliment of imitation. This imitation, however, was to prove its greatest danger. Its influence on German literature turned out to be disastrous: lacking the complexity of his character, missing his ambivalence, misunderstanding his irony, Heine's German imitators succumbed all too easily to those twin dangers of sentimentality and cynicism which their great model had—usually for legitimate purposes—deliberately skirted. Journalists and poetasters succeeded so well in imitating Heine's sometimes far from admirable mannerisms that they have almost obscured his achievement; and since the great attack on Heine by the Viennese satirist Karl Kraus—a kindred spirit if ever there was one, who could not, however, distinguish Heine from his imitators—Heine has been in disrepute even with those who cannot be suspected of racial or political prejudice. When in the year 1953 thirty men of letters eminent in different fields (among them Thomas Mann, Hermann Hesse, R. A. Schröder, Martin Buber, Karl Kerényi and Emil Staiger) were asked to name their favorite German poems, nearly every nineteenth-century poet of note was found to figure somewhere in their choice; but no one named a single poem by Heinrich Heine." S. S. Prawer, *op. cit.*, p. 9. Reprinted by permission.

11. "It cannot be denied that there are things in the *Buch der Lieder* which even seasoned readers of Heine's earlier poetry can hardly read without blenching" (*ibid.*, p. 40). Referring to the first verse of Song 14, Prawer continues: "How could the poet . . . have left unblotted those jingling and crassly sentimental lines . . . which betray an equal failure of sensibility and of ear?"

the words alone. I am inclined to think that the more a song depends upon textual interpretation by a singer, the less good it is. According to Jack M. Stein,[12] Goethe believed that the music of a song must not outweigh the poem, lest the music interfere with the verbal expression. I agree with Stein that in nineteenth-century song the "richness of musical setting" often makes the music more important than the words,[13] but so much less than regarding this consequence as a danger, I consider it the most desirable effect possible. Moreover, I have had no hesitation in making the music of *Dichterliebe* the almost exclusive subject of my analytic essay later in this volume.

To the extent that attention is paid to the words of *Dichterliebe*, Schumann is generally admired for the declamatory aspects of his settings. The musical accents correspond to the verbal meter, the right words are emphasized, the punctuation is observed (in the rests in the vocal part), the tempos permit ungarbled diction, and the accompaniments are not too heavy:

> Schumann, in his lieder and choral pieces, was the first of the Germans who troubled about correct declamation. Before him, neither in opera nor in simple songs did any one take offence at prosodical absurdities; and it is significant that Weber, Marschner, and Mendelssohn—educated men, and not devoid of humour—should have allowed so many anomalies to pass. The source of many a curious instance of obtuseness in this respect—composers, singers, and the public are alike implicated—may be sought in the fact that the tunes of German popular songs and chorales, from Luther's time downwards, were generally older, often much older, than the words. Throughout the history of music, and not in Germany alone, it has been a common practice to fit new words to old tunes—as, for instance, Moore [Irish poet and musician, 1779-1852] did in his *Irish Melodies*—and nobody seems to have cared whether or not the words and the tune meet on equal terms. To this, again, must be added the universal habit of singing successive stanzas to the same tune, as in the German Balladen of Zumsteeg and Zelter, or in many of the sea songs of Dibdin.[14]

12. Jack M. Stein, *Was Goethe Wrong about the Nineteenth-Century Lied? An Examination of the Relation of Poem and Music*, in *Publications of the Modern Language Association*, 77/3 (June, 1962), 239.

13. *Ibid.*, p. 236.

14. Edward Dannreuther, *The Romantic Period (Oxford History of Music*, Vol. 6), 2nd ed., Oxford, 1931, pp. 273–74 (reprinted by permission of Oxford University Press). A minority view toward Schumann's treatment of vocal texts is expressed by Hermann Bischoff: "Does it not seem as if the first four bars of this song [Song 2, *Dichterliebe*] had nothing to do with the poem, but rather that Schumann had sought out a poem to fit his [preconceived] musical ideas?" Cf. *Das deutsche Lied*, 2nd ed., 190?, p. 52.

On the other hand, there are those who feel that, because of the very nature of song, the declamation of a poem is necessarily spoiled. The English composer Michael Tippett has said: "The music of a song destroys the verbal music of a poem utterly."[15]

It is also generally felt that Schumann absorbed the spirit of Heine's poetry: the English writer J. A. Fuller-Maitland went so far as to state that "it is sometimes impossible to rid ourselves of the impression that the songs are the work of one man, not two. Not one of all those subtle touches of pathos, humour, or passion, which make Heine's poetry what it is, is lost upon Schumann . . ."[16]—but this is less easy to judge. Again, in the words of Michael Tippett: "The moment the composer begins to create the musical verses of his song, he destroys our appreciation of the poem as poetry, and substitutes an appreciation of his music as song."[17] According to Robert Haven Schauffler, Sir Henry Hadow is said to have believed that "to know Heine one must know Schumann's treatment of the *Buch der Lieder*." Schauffler continues: "He [Hadow] would have been more exact if he had written instead: 'To know how Heine can be manhandled, one must know, etc.' "[18]

How does one determine the spirit of a poem, and how does one judge the composer's sensitivity to it? Heine is said to have introduced much ironic wit into his poetry, and certainly one can easily detect the surprise ending in the sixth verse of Song 16. Schumann just as certainly noticed it and reflected it in the music, to the extent that he made a substantial change in the music that follows the fifth verse (cf. pp. 91-92 below.)

But what about Song 4? Here the alleged irony arises when the beloved's kiss is followed by bitter tears. Does this *dénouement* constitute genuine irony—possibly based on the assumption that the kiss was only imaginary—or is it merely a case of sentimental "weeping for joy"? And whatever our answer may be, how do we judge Schumann's response to the poem? According to Martin Cooper, Schumann appreciated the

15. Denis Stevens, ed., *A History of Song*, New York, 1960, p. 462.
16. J. A. Fuller-Maitland, *Robert Schumann*, London, 1884, p. 65.
17. *Op. cit.*, p. 462.
18. Robert Haven Schauffler, *Florestan, The Life and Works of Robert Schumann*, New York, 1945, pp. 385-86, footnote 10. Strange as this view may seem coming from an admirer of Schumann's songs, it reflects Schauffler's belief that song is generally an inferior type of music, "[to] be rated . . . on a lower artistic plane than instrumental music, because it is a sort of program music, and because it sabotages the word-melody and harmony of verse" (p. 388). Schumann himself held a similar view at one time; cf. the discussion of his letter to Hermann Hirschbach, p. 126, below.

ironic ending, but subtly avoided any obvious musical correlation with the verbal emotion.[19] I am inclined to beg the question; and in any case, I think that the music of Song 4 is more interesting than the words.[20] However, this is not to say that the words are an inessential part of the total auditory experience of the songs; certainly there is a real objection to replacing the original German texts with translations, on the grounds that it would interfere with one's purely *musical* appreciation of the songs.

Of course, the subject of the relation of words and music is an extremely difficult one, to which I can hardly do justice here. The controversy is nowhere clearer than in the evaluation of one of the most notable aspects of *Dichterliebe*—the extended piano postludes, which appear in no less than eight of the songs (5, 6, 8, 9, 10, 11, 12, and 16).[21] When the songs first appeared, Schumann was criticized for the prominence of the piano parts, but the postludes subsequently won approval. In the view of August Reissman, the postludes are called for by the pregnant endings of the Heine verses.[22] But from another point of view, the postludes indicate how little the words count—else what purpose in so much non-verbal music? Another issue relating to words and music is the generally consistent piano figuration found in many of the songs. From one standpoint, the figuration creates and maintains the atmosphere of a song, representing the mood of the text; from another, the figuration serves musical purposes exclusively, and its very inflexibility detracts from the variety of word nuances within the several verses of the poem.

Dichterliebe is probably the most popular of Schumann's song cycles[23]—if not the most popular of all song cycles as well. This popu-

19. Cf. Martin Cooper, *The Songs*, in Gerald Abraham, ed., *Schumann, A Symposium*, London, 1952, pp. 106-07.

20. In fact, the words actually impede my enjoyment of the whole cycle—to the extent that I heed them. The moping, distraught lover portrayed in German song cycles bores me, but this feeling in no way detracts from my enthusiasm for the music of the great song cycles of Beethoven, Schubert, and Schumann.

21. The postlude of Song 16 recapitulates the postlude of Song 12, a minor third higher. In another well-known song cycle, *Frauenliebe und -Leben*, Schumann repeats part of the first song in the final postlude, following a practice initiated by Beethoven in what is generally regarded as the first song cycle, *An die ferne Geliebte*.

22. "Furthermore, the poet reveals such broad perspectives in the endings [of his poems] that the composer who strives to enter fully into the mood of the poet is forced to [employ] greatly extended postludes." Cf. *Robert Schumann, sein Leben und seine Werke*, 3rd ed., Berlin, 1879, pp. 85-86.

23. An exception to this view is found in Elizabeth Schumann's book *German Song*. New York, 1948. On page 32, she states that she prefers *Frauenliebe und -Leben*,

larity rests, I believe, on the rather cheerful, pretty quality of the songs; even the settings of the sad or serious poems are not very severe. The *Liederkreis*, Op. 39, as well as some of the later songs such as Op. 89 and Op. 135, have a much more sombre character, which requires more familiarity to appreciate—or so I have found; *Dichterliebe*, on the other hand, is extremely accessible for most listeners at first hearing.

Among Schumann's larger cycles, I would say that *Dichterliebe* competes for first place mainly with the Eichendorff *Liederkreis*, Op. 39.[24] For true interdependence of voice and piano, Op. 39 is superior to *Dichterliebe*, the postludes of the latter notwithstanding: the piano accompaniments that occur *simultaneously* with the voices in Op. 39 exhibit more independence and are of generally greater interest than the accompaniments of *Dichterliebe*.

In another respect, however, *Dichterliebe* is superior to Op. 39: most of the songs of the former cycle are so brief and quiet—so unsubstantial—that they emerge quite clearly as dependent parts of an inclusive whole. Observe the brevity of Song 3; the absence of the prevailing tonic triad at the beginning of Songs 1, 5, 9, 12 and 14; and the harmonically inconclusive endings of Songs 1, 2, 4, 8, 9, and 13. Only at the end of the cycle is the episodic quality of these songs replaced—quite appropriately—by the greater length and substance of the two terminal songs, *Aus alten Märchen* and *Die alten, bösen Lieder*.

---

and in particular believes that *Ein Jüngling liebt ein Mädchen* and *Aus alten Märchen* "are instances of the student-song mediocrity which seems to me a lapse from [Schumann's] own standard." Ernst Bücken, a German writing in the Nazi period, considers the music of the *Liederkreis*, Op. 39, superior to *Dichterliebe*, apparently more because of his wish to disavow the Jewish Heine than because of any genuine critical judgment. Cf. *Das deutsche Lied*, Hamburg, 1939, p. 99. See also footnote 24, below.

24. *Frauenliebe und -Leben (A Woman's Love and Life)* runs a close third. Philip L. Miller says: ". . . fond as one may become of Schumann's *Frauenliebe und -Leben* cycle, one admires it less than the *Dichterliebe*, not simply because the music of the one is superior to the other—beyond question Heine was a finer poet than Chamisso. Nowadays one does not take *Frauenliebe* too seriously because of the text—*Così non fan tutte*." (*The Ring of Words*, New York, 1963, p. xv. Reprinted by permission of Doubleday & Company, Inc.) I agree with Miller that the music is not up to that of *Dichterliebe*, but feel that the problem with the poetry is not so much its quality as, in the words of Martin Cooper, its subject: "Certainly the humble adoration of the chosen male that breathes from the poems of Chamisso . . . wakes very little echo in a modern listener . . . It is a very welcome change to move on to the quite unmatrimonial sentiments of Heine . . ." (*The Songs*, in Gerald Abraham, ed., *Schumann, A Symposium*, London, 1952, p. 104. Reprinted by permission of Oxford University Press). In my view, the quality of the music remains central, however; the individual songs of *Frauenliebe* do not have the beauty of some of the songs of Op. 39 nor are they so short and dependent as the songs of *Dichterliebe*.

THE SCORE OF DICHTERLIEBE

Contents

DICHTERLIEBE

Langsam, zart.

1.

Im wun _ derschö _ nen Mo _ nat Mai, als al _ le Knos _ pen

sprangen, da ist in mei _ nem Her _ zen die Lie _ be auf _ ge _ gan _ gen.

ritard.

Im wunderschönen Monat Mai,
Als alle Knospen sprangen,
Da ist in meinem Herzen
Die Liebe aufgegangen.

Im wunderschönen Monat Mai,
Als alle Vögel sangen,
Da hab' ich ihr gestanden
Mein Sehnen und Verlangen.

In the lovely month of May,
when all the buds were bursting,
then within my heart
love broke forth.

In the lovely month of May,
when all the birds were singing,
then I confessed to her
my longing and desire.

Aus meinen Thränen spriessen
Viel blühende Blumen hervor,
Und meine Seufzer werden
Ein Nachtigallenchor,

Und wenn du mich lieb hast Kindchen,
Schenk' ich dir die Blumen all',
Und vor deinem Fenster soll klingen
Das Lied der Nachtigall.

From my tears spring up
many blooming flowers,
and my sighs become
a chorus of nightingales.

And if you love me, child,
I give you all the flowers,
and before your window shall sound
the song of the nightingale.

Die Rose, die Lilie, die Taube,
      die Sonne,
Die liebt' ich einst alle in Liebeswonne,
Ich lieb' sie nicht mehr, ich liebe
      alleine
Die Kleine, die Feine, die Reine,
      die Eine;
Sie selber, aller Liebe Bronne
Ist Rose und Lilie und Taube und
      Sonne.

The rose, the lily, the dove, the sun—
I once loved them all with ecstatic love.
I love them no more, I love only
the little one, the dainty one, the pure
      one, the One.
She alone, the well-spring of all love,
is rose and lily and dove and sun.

Wenn ich in deine Augen seh',
So schwindet all' mein Leid und Weh;
Doch wenn ich küsse deinen Mund,
So werd' ich ganz und gar gesund.

Wenn ich mich lehn' an deine Brust,
Kommt's über mich wie Himmelslust;
Doch wenn du sprichst: Ich liebe dich,
So muss ich weinen bitterlich.

When I look into your eyes
all my sorrow and pain disappear;
but when I kiss your mouth,
then I become wholly well.

When I lie upon your breast
a heavenly happiness comes over me;
but when you say: I love you!
then I must weep bitterly.

Dein Angesicht, so lieb und schön,
Das hab' ich jüngst im Traum geseh'n.
Es ist so mild und engelgleich,
Und doch so bleich, so schmerzenreich.

Und nur die Lippen, die sind roth;
Bald aber küsst sie bleich der Tod,
Erlöschen wird das Himmelslicht,
Das aus den frommen Augen bricht.

Your face so dear and beautiful
I have seen lately in my dream;
it is so gentle and angelic
and yet so pale, so full of pain.

And only the lips, they are red;
but soon death kisses them pale.
Extinguished is the heavenly light
that breaks forth from the gentle eyes.

Lehn' deine Wang' an meine Wang',
Dann fliessen die Thränen zusammen,
Und an mein Herz drück' fest dein Herz,

Dann schlagen zusammen die Flammen.

Und wenn in die grosse Flamme fliesst
Der Strom von unsern Thränen,
Und wenn dich mein Arm gewaltig
    umschliesst,
Sterb' ich vor Liebessehnen!

Lay your cheek upon my cheek,
then our tears will flow together;
and press your heart firmly against
    my heart,
then the flames of our passion will beat
    together.

And if on the great flames flows
the stream of our tears
and if my arm clasps you powerfully,

I die of love's desire.

Ich will meine Seele tauchen
In den Kelch der Lilie hinein,
Die Lilie soll klingend hauchen
Ein Lied von der Liebsten mein.

Das Lied soll schauern und beben
Wie der Kuss von ihrem Mund',
Den sie mir einst gegeben
In wunderbar süsser Stund'!

I will dip my soul
into the chalice of the lily;
the lily shall breath
a song about my beloved.

The song shall quiver and palpitate
like the kiss of her mouth
that once she gave me
in a wonderfully sweet moment.

Ziemlich langsam.

6.

Im Rhein, im hei - li - gen Stro - me, da spie - gelt sich in den Well'n, mit sei - nem gros - sen Do - me das gros - se, hei - li - ge Köln. Im Dom, da steht ein Bild - niss auf gol - de - nem Le - der ge - malt. In mei - nes Le - bens Wild - niss hat's freund - lich hin - ein ge - strahlt. Es schweben Blu - men und Eng - lein um

Im Rhein, im heiligen Strome,
Da spiegelt sich in den Well'n,
Mit seinem grossen Dome
Das grosse, heilige Köln.

Im Dom, da steht ein Bildniss
Auf goldenem Leder gemalt.
In meines Lebens Wildniss
Hat's freundlich hineingestrahlt.

Es schweben Blumen und Englein
Um unsre Liebe Frau,
Die Augen, die Lippen, die Wänglein,
Die gleichen der Liebsten genau.

The Rhine, the holy river,
reflects in its waves,
with its great cathedral,
the great holy city of Cologne.

In the cathedral there hangs a painting
painted on gilded leather;
in the confusion of my life
it has shone kindly down upon me.

Flowers and cherubs float
about Our dear Lady.
Her eyes, her lips, her cheeks
are exactly like those of my love.

Ich grolle nicht und wenn das Herz
    auch bricht.
Ewig verlor'nes Lieb, ich grolle nicht.
Wie du auch strahlst in
    Diamantenpracht,
Es fällt kein Strahl in deines
    Herzens Nacht.

Das weiss ich längst. Ich sah dich ja im
    Traume,
Und sah die Nacht in deines Herzens
    Raume,
Und sah die Schlang', die dir am
    Herzen frisst,
Ich sah, mein Lieb, wie sehr du elend
    bist.

I bear no grudge, even though my
    heart may break,
eternally lost love! I bear no grudge.
However you may shine in the
    splendor of your diamonds,
no ray of light falls in the darkness
    of your heart.

I have long known this. I saw you in
    a dream,
and saw the night within the void of
    your heart,
and saw the serpent that is eating
    your heart—
I saw, my love, how very miserable
    you are.

8.

Und wüs-stens die Blu-men die klei-nen, wie tief ver-wun-det mein Herz, sie wür-den mit mir

6

wei-nen zu hei-len mei-nen Schmerz. Und

wüs-stens die Nach-ti-gal-len, wie ich so trau-rig und

12

krank, sie lies-sen fröh-lich er-schal-len er-

Und wüssten's die Blumen die kleinen,   And if the flowers knew, the little ones,

Wie tief verwundet mein Herz,   how deeply my heart is wounded,
Sie würden mit mir weinen   they would weep with me
Zu heilen meinen Schmerz.   to heal my affliction.

Und wüssten's die Nachtigallen,   And if the nightingales knew
Wie ich so traurig und krank,   how sad and sick I am.
Sie liessen fröhlich erschallen   they would cheerfully sound forth
Erquickenden Gesang.   their comforting song.

Und wüssten sie mein Wehe,   And if my woes were known
Die goldnen Sternelein,   to the golden stars,
Sie kämen aus ihrer Höhe,   they would come down from their heights

Und sprächen Trost mir ein.   and speak consolation to me.

Sie alle können's nicht wissen,   They cannot understand it;
Nur Eine kennt meinen Schmerz: only one knows my suffering:
Sie hat ja selbst zerrissen,   she herself, indeed, has broken,
Zerrissen mir das Herz.   broken my heart.

Nicht zu rasch.

Das ist ein Flö ten und Gei _ _ gen, Trom _ pe _ _ ten schmet _ tern da rein, _____ Trom _ pe _ ten schmettern da _ rein. Da tanzt wohl im Hoch _ zeit rei _ _ _ gen die Herz _ al _ ler _ lieb _ ste mein,

Das ist ein Flöten und Geigen,
Trompetten schmettern darein.
Da tanzt wohl im Hochzeitreigen
Die Herzallerliebste mein.

Das ist ein Klingen und Dröhnen,
Ein Pauken und ein Schalmein;
Dazwischen schluchzen and stöhnen
Die lieblichen Engelein.

There is playing of flutes and fiddles,
trumpets blaring forth;
there in the wedding party
my dearest love is dancing.

There is sounding and roaring
of drums and pipes
and in the midst of it
the dear angels sob and groan.

Hör' ich das Liedchen klingen,
Das einst die Liebste sang,
So will mir die Brust zerspringen
Von wildem Schmerzendrang.

Es treibt mich ein dunkles Sehnen
Hinauf zur Waldeshöh',
Dort löst sich auf in Thränen
Mein übergrosses Weh.

When I hear the song
that once my sweetheart sang,
my heart wants to burst
from the stress of savage pain.

An oppressive longing drives me
up to the wooded hilltop;
there I find release in tears
from my intolerable grief.

11.

Ein Jüngling liebt ein
　　Mädchen,
Die hat einen andern erwählt,
Der And're liebt eine And're,
Und hat sich mit dieser vermählt.

Das Mädchen nimmt aus Ärger
Den ersten, besten Mann,
Der ihr in den Weg gelaufen,
Der Jüngling ist übel dran.

Es ist eine alte Geschichte,
Doch bleibt sie immer neu,
Und wem sie just passiret,
Dem bricht das Herz entzwei.

A boy loves a girl

who has chosen another;
the other loves still another
and has married this one.

The girl takes out of spite
the first, most eligible man
who comes her way;
the boy is miserable over it.

It is an old story,
yet it remains ever new;
and whoever experiences it,
has his heart broken in two.

Ziemlich langsam.

Am leuch _ tenden Som _ mer _ morgen geh' ich im Gar _ ten her _ um. Es

flü _ stern und spre _ chen die Blu _ _ men, ich a _ ber wand _ le

stumm. Es flü _ stern und spre _ chen die Blumen und

schau'n mit _ lei _ dig mich au: Sei uns_rer Schwester nicht bö _ _ se, du

langsamer

Am leuchtenden Sommermorgen
Geh' ich im Garten herum.
Es flüstern und sprechen die Blumen,

Ich aber wandle stumm.

Es flüstern und sprechen die Blumen

Und schau'n mitleidig mich an:
Sei unserer Schwester nicht böse,
Du trauriger blasser Mann!

In the bright summer morning
I walk about the garden.
The flowers are whispering
    and talking,
but I wander in silence.

The flowers are whispering
    and talking,
and they look pityingly at me:
"Don't be angry with our sister,
you doleful, pale man."

Phantastisch, markirt.

[12a]

leuch_tet mei_ne Lie _ be in ih _ rer dunkeln Pracht, wie'n Mär _ chen,traurig und trü _ be, er_

zählt in der Som_mernacht. Im Zau _ ber_gar_ten wal _ len zwei Buh _ len stumm und al _ lein, es

singen die Nach_ti_gal _ len, es flimmert der Mon_denschein. Die Jung _ frau steht still wie ein

Bild _ niss. Der Rit _ ter vor _ ihr kniet. Da

kommt __ der Rie _ se der Wild _ niss, die ban _ ge Jung _ frau

flieht.

Der Rit _ ter sinkt blu _ tend zur Er _ de, es

stolpert der Riese nach Haus, __ es stol _ pert der Rie _ se nach Haus. Wenn ich be _

gra _ ben wer_de, dann ist das Mär _ chen aus.

Es leuchtet meine Liebe
In ihrer dunkeln Pracht,
Wie'n Märchen, traurig und trübe,
Erzählt in der Sommernacht.

Im Zaubergarten wallen
Zwei Buhlen stumm und allein,
Es singen die Nachtigallen,
Es flimmert der Mondenschein.

Die Jungfrau steht still wie ein
    Bildniss.
Der Ritter vor ihr kniet.
Da kommt der Riese der Wildniss,
Die bange Jungfrau flieht.

Der Ritter sinkt blutend zur Erde,
Es stolpert der Riese nach Haus
Wenn ich begraben werde,
Dann ist das Märchen aus.

My love shines
in its dark splendor
like a tale, sad and troubled,
told on a summer night.

"In the magic garden wander
two lovers, silent and alone;
the nightingales sing,
the moonlight glimmers.

The girl stands still as a statue,

the knight kneels before her.
The giant of the wilderness appears;
the frightened girl flees.

The knight sinks bloody to the earth,
the giant stumbles homeward—"
When I am buried
then the tale will be finished.

Da grüss_en drei Schat _ ten _ ge _ stal _ _ _ _ ten kopf _ ni _ ckend zum Wa _ gen, zum Wa _ gen her _ ein, sie hüp _ fen und schneiden Ge _ sich _ ter so spöt _ tisch und doch so scheu und quir _ len wie Ne_bel zu _ sam _ men und ki _ chern und huschen vor _ bei.

Mein Wagen rollet langsam
Durch lustiges Waldesgrün,
Durch blumige Thäler, die zaubrisch
Im Sonnenglanze blüh'n.

Ich sitze und sinne und träume
Und denk' an die Liebste mein.
Da grüssen drei Schattengestalten
Kopfnickend zum Wagen herein,

Sie hüpfen und schneiden Gesichter
So spöttisch und doch so scheu
Und quirlen wie Nebel zusammen
Und kichern und huschen vorbei.

My carriage moves slowly
through the gay forest green,
through flowery valleys, that magically
bloom in the splendor of summer.

I sit and meditate and dream
and think of my beloved;
three shadow-forms greet me,
nodding into the carriage.

They hop and make faces,
so mocking and yet so shy,
and whirl together like clouds,
and chuckle and glide past.

Ich hab' im Traum geweinet.
Mir träumte, du lägest im Grab.
Ich wachte auf, und die Thräne
Floss noch von der Wange herab.

Ich hab' im Traum geweinet.
Mir träumt', du verliessest mich.
Ich wachte auf, und ich weinte
Noch lange bitterlich.

Ich hab' im Traum geweinet,
Mir träumte, du wärst mir noch gut.
Ich wachte auf und noch immer
Strömt meine Thränenfluth.

I cried in my dream:
I dreamed that you lay in your grave.
I woke up, and the tears
were still streaming down my cheeks.

I cried in my dream:
I dreamed that you had forsaken me.
I woke up, and I cried
still long and bitterly.

I cried in my dream:
I dreamed that you still loved me.
I woke up, and still
the flood of my tears is streaming.

14.

All — nächt — lich im Trau — me seh' ich dich, und

se — he dich freundlich, freund — lich grüssen, und laut aufweinend stürz' ich mich zu

ritard.

dei — nen süs — sen Füs — sen.   Du sie — hest mich

an weh — mü — thig — lich, und schüt — telst, schüt — telst das

blon — de Köpfchen; aus dei — nen Au — gen schlei — chen sich die Per — len — thrä — nen —

Allnächtlich im Traume seh' ich dich,
Und sehe dich freundlich grüssen,
Und laut aufweinend stürz' ich mich
Zu deinen süssen Füssen.

Du siehest mich an wehmüthiglich,
Und schüttelst das blonde Köpfchen;
Aus deinen Augen schleichen sich
Die Perlenthränentröpfchen.

Du sagst mir heimlich ein leises Wort,

Und gibst mir den Strauss von
      Cypressen,
Ich wache auf, und der Strauss ist fort
Und's Wort hab ich vergessen.

Every night in my dreams I see you,
and see your friendly greeting;
and, loudly weeping, I throw myself
at your sweet feet.

You look at me sadly
and shake your little blond head;
from your eyes steal
teardrops like pearls.

You murmur intimately a quiet word
      to me,
and give me a spray of cypress.

I wake up and the spray is gone
and I have forgotten the word.

Aus al _ ten Märchen winkt es her _ vor mit weis_ser Hand, da

singt es und da klingt es von ei _ nem Zau_ber_land, wo buu_te Blu_men blü _ hen im

goldnen A _ bend_licht und lieb_lich duf_tend glü _ hen mit bräut_lichem Ge _ sicht.

Und grü_ne Bäu_me sin _ gen ur_

Aus alten Märchen winkt es	Out of the old fairy tales
Hervor mit weisser Hand,	a white hand beckons;
Da singt es und da klingt es	there are singing and sounding
Von einem Zauberland,	from a magic country
Wo bunte Blumen blühen	where bright flowers bloom
Im goldnen Abendlicht	in the golden evening light,
Und lieblich duftend glühen	and in their lovely fragrance glow
Mit bräutlichem Gesicht.	like a visage of a bride;
Und grüne Bäume singen	and green trees sing
Uralte Melodei'n,	ancient melodies;
Die Lüfte heimlich klingen	the breezes sound peacefully,
Und Vögel schmettern drein	and the birds warble there;
Und Nebelbilder steigen	and hazy images rise up
Wohl aus der Erd' hervor	from the earth
Und tanzen luft'gen Reigen	and dance airy revels
Im wunderlichen Chor,	in a mystical chorus;
Und blaue Funken brennen	and blue sparks burn
An jedem Blatt und Reis,	on every leaf and twig,
Und rothe Lichter rennen	and red lights rush about
Im irren, wirren Kreis,	in confused, fantastic circles;
Und bunte Quellen brechen	and noisy springs burst forth
Aus wildem Marmorstein,	out of rough marble,
Und seltsam in den Bächen	and strangely in the streams
Strahlt fort der Wiederschein.	the reflection shines forth.
Ach könnt' ich dorthin kommen	Ah, could I go there,
Und dort mein Herz erfreu'n,	and there delight my heart,
Und aller Qual entnommen	removed from all torment,
Und frei und selig sein!	and be free and blessed!
Ach, jenes Land der Wonne,	Ah, that land of rapture,
Das seh' ich oft im Traum,	I often see it in dreams,
Doch kommt die Morgensonne,	but when the morning rises
Zerfliesst's wie eitel Schaum.	it vanishes like spraying foam.

wie zu Mainz die Brück'. Und holt mir auch zwölf Rie _ sen, die müs_sen noch stär _ ker

sein, als wie der star _ ke Chri _ stoph im Dom zu Köln am

Rhein. Die sol _ len den Sarg fort _ tra_gen, und sen_ken in's Meer hin_ab; denn

sol _ chem gros _ sen Sar _ ge ge _ bührt ein gros _ ses Grab.

Wisst ihr wa_rum der Sarg wohl so gross und schwer mag sein?_____ Ich

senkt' auch mei _ ne   Lie _ be   und   mei _ nen Schmerz hin _ ein!

Die alten, bösen Lieder,	The old evil songs,

Die alten, bösen Lieder,
Die Träume bös bos' und arg,
Die lasst uns jetzt begraben,
Holt einen grossen Sarg.

Hinein leg' ich gar Manches,
Doch sag' ich noch nicht was.
Der Sarg muss sein noch grösser,
Wie's Heidelberger Fass.

Und holt eine Todtenbahre
Und Breter fest und dick
Auch muss sie sein noch länger,
Als wie zu Mainz die Brück'.

Und holt mir auch zwölf Riesen,
Die müssen noch stärker sein,
Als wie der starke Christoph
Im Dom zu Köln am Rhein.

Die sollen den Sarg forttragen,
Und senken in's Meer hinab;
Denn solchem grossen Sarge
Gebührt ein grosses Grab.

Wisst ihr warum der Sarg wohl
So gross und schwer mag sein?
Ich senkt' auch meine Liebe
Und meinen Schmerz hinein!

The old evil songs,
the wicked, depraved dreams,
let us bury them now;
fetch a large coffin.

Therein I will put a great deal,
but I won't say yet of what;
the coffin must be even larger
than the Heidelberg Cask.

And fetch a bier
of strong thick boards;
they must also be even longer
than the bridge at Mainz.

And fetch me, too, twelve giants;
they must be even stronger
than strong Christopher
in the cathedral at Cologne on the
        Rhine.

They shall bear the coffin out
and sink it into the sea,
for such a large coffin
deserves a large grave.

Do you know why the coffin
must be so large and heavy?
I have also sunk my love
and my suffering in it.

Textual Note

Dichterliebe originally consisted of twenty songs, four of which were omitted in the first edition, published in two volumes by Peters, Leipzig, 1844 (plate no. 2867). Schumann actually offered all of the songs to the Peters publishing firm, under the title *Twenty Lieder by H. Heine*, Op. 47, and only subsequently removed four of the songs and added the title *Dichterliebe*.[1] In his *Projectenbuch*, begun in December 1840, Schumann includes *Dichterliebe, 16 Lieder v. Heine* under the year 1840, and fails to mention the extra four songs in the remainder of the "project-book", which goes up to 1853.[2] In the present edition, the four omitted songs are included in their original order, but numbered in such a way as to preserve the final numbering of the sixteen remaining songs (thus, Songs 4a and 4b were originally Songs 5 and 6, and Songs 12a and 12b were originally Songs 15 and 16). All four songs were eventually published: 4a and 12a as Nos. 2 and 3 of Op. 127 (Wilhelm Paul, Dresden, 1854, plate no. 462), and 4b and 12b as Nos. 2 and 4 of Op. 142 (Rieter-Biedermann, Leipzig and Winterthur, 1858, plate no. 42.)[3] When follow-

1. According to Jansen; cf. *Robert Schumanns Briefe, Neue Folge*, 2nd ed., Leipzig, 1904, p. 540.

2. Cf. G. Eismann, *Robert Schumann, Ein Quellenwerk über sein Leben und Schaffen*, 2 vols., Leipzig, 1956, I, 147ff. I have been unable to locate any documentation concerning Schumann's reasons for omitting the four songs. I suggest some of the potential reasons in the analytic essay which follows the score.

3. Although the composer's manuscript, containing all 20 songs, has been available in the Deutsche Staatsbibliothek (formerly the Königlichen Bibliothek zu Berlin) since 1904 (and its whereabouts prior to that date were not unknown), many writers have apparently believed the extra four songs to be among Schumann's last song compositions. Even Friedländer (cf. p. 59), who had access to the manuscript, gives the date of composition of *Dein Angesicht* as 1850-51. The error has been perpetuated in recent publications, including *Die Musik in Geschichte und Gegenwart*, Kassel, 1965, which gives the composition date of Op. 142 as 1852 (XII, 295), and in *Grove's Dictionary* (1954) which dates all four songs from 1850 or later (VII, 637). However, Gerald Abraham, the author of the Schumann article in *Grove's*, correctly

ing a recording of *Dichterliebe* with this edition, the reader is cautioned that the extra four songs are not included in any known recordings, so he must be prepared to skip directly from Song 4 to 5, and from 12 to 13. (Of the four extra songs, only 4a, *Dein Angesicht*, is at all well-known.)

This edition has been prepared from four sources: 1) a microfilm copy of the composer's manuscript, for which I am indebted to Dr. Karl-Heinz Köhler, Director of the Music Division of the Deutsche Staatsbibliothek, Berlin (DDR); 2) the first editions, copies of which were provided courtesy of the Brown Collection of the Boston Public Library; 3) the Schumann Gesamtausgabe, Ser. 13, Vol. II, No. 13, edited by Clara Schumann and published by Breitkopf & Härtel, Leipzig, 1885; and 4) the current Peters edition of Schumann's songs, Vol. 1, edited by Max Friedländer (190?), and Vol. 3, edited by A. Dörffel (188?). Since Schumann is reported to have habitually corrected proofs right up to the date of publication,4 I have generally relied on the first editions.5

---

describes the four songs as part of the original twenty (*ibid.*, p. 611).

All of these errors have led to some rather amusing comparisons between the styles of early and supposedly late Schumann songs. Thus, J. A. Fuller-Maitland demonstrated a knack for spotting stylistic resemblances in his *Robert Schumann*, p. 66, where he mentions that the "idyllic grace" of many of the *Dichterliebe* songs is re-echoed, among other places, in *Dein Angesicht;* he also cites a resemblance between *Das ist ein Flöten und Geigen* (Song 9) and *Es leuchtet meine Liebe* (Song 12a), which he also points out as the basis for the Scherzo of Schumann's String Quartet in A minor. More recently, Hans Redlich, writing in the January 1951 issue of *The Monthly Musical Record*, p. 16, reluctantly acknowledges the early origin of *Mein Wagen rollet langsam* (Song 12b), but thinks Schumann must have revised it during the winter of 1853-54: "To me personally it seems inconceivable that a song like *Mein Wagen*, with its morbid lack of contrast and its obsessional repetitiveness in the piano part, could represent a conception of the most creative and inspired year in Schumann's life." However, comparison with the manuscript shows virtually no difference between the 1840 version and the one printed in 1858. Finally, Eric Werba has written that at the end of Schumann's life "the deathly ill musician . . . looked back to his earlier mastery in a Heine poem, *Dein Angesicht*" (*Das Schumann-Lied in der Gegenwart*, in *Österreichische Musikzeitschrift*, XI [1956], 212).

4. "[The proof reader, Roitzsch,] told me that Schumann unceasingly polished and altered his works when checking the proofs. [Roitzsch] particularly noticed that Schumann made numerous changes in the proofs of Op. 48 [*Dichterliebe*] and then returned to the first version in the final proof-reading." Cf. Hermann Erler, *Robert Schumanns Leben aus seinem Briefen*, 2 vols. Berlin, 1887, II, 124. Also see Viktor Ernst Wolff, *Lieder Robert Schumanns in ersten und späteren Fassungen*, Leipzig, 1914, pp. 20-21.

Schumann's Op. 142 was published posthumously, of course, but there is some testimony to suggest that Schumann may have prepared the first edition himself at an earlier date. Cf. H. F. Redlich, *Schumann Discoveries, A Postscript*, in *Monthly Musical Record*, LXXXI (Jan. 1951), 16.

5. In one important case I have rejected all of the cited editions in favor of the manuscript. In the published versions of Song 13, m. 18, the voice part has a quarter rest and eighth rest, followed by three eighth notes (G♭); in the manuscript, the

Where these differ from the Gesamtausgabe, I have consulted the manuscript and Friedländer-Dörffel. Most of the differences in the published versions hinge on details of dynamics, accents, phrasing, and the like; only one pitch comes into question.[6] For verbal punctuation and capitalizations, I have consulted the Schumann manuscript and the first edition, rather than the original Heine texts; and similarly I have restored the original Heine words only where the variants in the song texts appear clearly inadvertent.[7]

The English translations that accompany the sixteen songs of *Dichterliebe* are drawn (with necessary adaptations corresponding to Schumann's alterations in Heine's texts) from *The Ring of Words: An Anthology of Song Texts*, translated, with an introduction, by Philip L. Miller, New York, 1963, pp. 40-45. (Reprinted by permission of Doubleday & Company, Inc.) Mr. Miller kindly provided the translations of the extra four songs especially for this edition.

---

second voice note is unmistakably a quarter note. The confusion arises from the fact that Schumann put one beat too many in the measure, by starting with three beats of rest instead of two. That he intended for the syllable "wach" to occur at the fourth beat seems clear both from the vertical alignment of the voice and piano parts, and by analogy with measure 7.

6. In the first edition and the Gesamtausgabe, the final top note of the penultimate measure of Song 12a is given as G instead of the more likely A. (The manuscript is unclear; Dörffel gives the A.)

7. 1) In Song 3, line 5, the original "Bronne" is replaced by "Wonne" in all the published editions; the MS clearly shows "Bronne"; 2) in Song 12a, line 11, "Ritter" occurs in the MS in place of "Riese," which is necessary for the narrative to make sense; 3) in Song 12b, line 7, Schumann clearly wrote "grüssen," not "huschen" as it appears in the published versions; in line 9, Schumann appears to have written "huschen," but again the sense of the poem requires Heine's original "hüpfen." Only the third "huschen" (line 12) of the published versions is correct; 4) the last word of the last verse of Song 15 is "Traum" in the MS and first edition—clearly an inadvertent substitute for "Schaum"; 5) the rhyme scheme, Song 16, verse 3, is spoiled by the interchange of the words "dick" and "fest" in the MS and first edition; "dick" should be the second word. to rhyme with "Brück."

ESSAYS IN ANALYSIS

Unless specified otherwise, all numbered footnotes in the following essays are those of the author.

ARTHUR KOMAR

~~~~~

The Music of Dichterliebe: *The Whole and Its Parts*

Do the songs of *Dichterliebe* constitute an integrated musical totality, or are they merely sixteen disjunct pieces? In some respects, a totality is implied by the way the songs are usually performed: the individual songs are rarely heard outside the cycle; when the cycle is programmed, none of the songs is omitted and their order is left intact; and audiences are expected to refrain from applause between songs. On the other hand, singers (and publishers) alter the keys of individual songs without concern for the original key relationships of the cycle. Surely a song cycle with key relationships so trivial that they can be varied with each performance—as in quasi-chance music—is a dubious musical totality!

In the following essay I shall assume that *Dichterliebe* is a single entity, and will attempt to determine in what respect and to what extent it constitutes an integrated musical whole. Before proceeding, let us consider seven possible conclusions to which our investigations might lead.

1) The songs are typical examples of Schumann's early lied style, are similar in length, and are based on poems that are alike in style, construction, and subject matter. Thus, the *Dichterliebe* songs belong together just as much as—but no more than—any other collection of Schumann's early brief love songs on texts by German Romantic poets.

2) The songs of *Dichterliebe* are similar to each other with respect to thematic segments, harmonic progressions, and rhythmic figurations. In number and kind, these similarities exceed the coincidental similarities to be found among any random collection of mid-nineteenth-century songs, and therefore they must be regarded as individual features of this particular collection. By way of example: Songs 2 and 13 open with an initial note repeated four times prior to the attack of a note a half-step higher and a return to the original note (Ex. 1); Songs 4 and 13 contain passages that are melodically equivalent, the final chord in each

case being a first-inversion minor triad (Ex. 2) ; Songs 5 and 8 are characterized by consistent thirty-second-note motion; and a transposed repetition of the greater part of the postlude of Song 12 is found in the postlude of Song 16.

Ex. 1   a) Song 2   b) Song 13

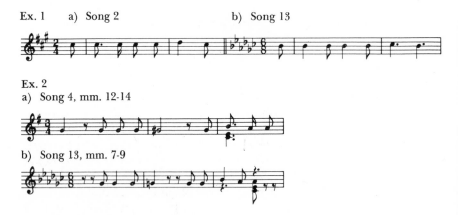

Ex. 2
a) Song 4, mm. 12-14

b) Song 13, mm. 7-9

3) The songs are related as in category 2), in addition to which some of the similar pitch configurations are untransposed. Again, examples are easy to find: compare the opening eight measures of Song 5 with mm. 9-12 of Song 1; the harmonic-melodic content of Song 2, mm. 12-14, with Song 16, mm. 47-49; and the G♭-major prolongations in Song 11, mm. 29-30 and Song 13, mm. 28-31. In both categories 2) and 3), the evidence supports the grouping of the songs together but does not justify the specific order of the songs within the cycle.

4) The pairing of songs within *Dichterliebe* is justified by elements of local continuity in adjacent songs. For example, the sequence of keys in Songs 2–3 (A major–D major) is prepared by the tonicization of D major in Song 2 (Ex. 3). And notice how the postlude of Song 8 is "repeated" in the introduction of Song 9.

Ex. 3   Song 2, mm. 12-13

D Major: V ——————— I
A Major: I ——————— IV —— I

5) The keys of the songs constitute a coherent key scheme, as indicated in *Dichterliebe* by the frequency of descending-fifth and -third motions from one song key to the next. (I should hesitate to place too much emphasis on key relationships alone, for one could put together an equally "coherent" song collection merely by picking any sixteen songs in the same ordered set of keys. In conjunction with categories 2), 3), and 4), however, category 5) represents a significant integration of compositional elements throughout a song cycle.)

6) A general compositional plan embraces all of the songs of the cycle in their given order. This category is superior to category 4) in that it includes a rationale for the ordering of non-adjacent songs with respect to each other, and goes beyond category 5) in supplying a rationale for the point at which the cycle concludes.

[To my knowledge, no one has authoritatively accounted for the way in which the movements of a large-scale work cohere. Schenker provided a theory of tonal music according to which the basic harmonic-melodic progression (*Ursatz*) of a piece controls the entire piece. But he applied this theory to individual movements rather than to entire cyclical works, and there is no way of distinguishing the *Ursatz* of a single movement from that of a complete (one-movement) work. And the school of motivic analysis represented by writers like Rudolph Réti[1] generally rests content with demonstrating motivic similarities without justifying ordering relationships. But if the movements of a sonata or symphony, or the songs of a cycle, belong together in a particular order, then some sort of controlling compositional plan must be demonstrated for them. An inkling of a general compositional plan for *Dichterliebe* is suggested by the consistent progress in the harmonic support for the pitch B in Songs 1-5; featured first as a dissonance in Song 1, B is generally consonant in Songs 2 and 3, becomes a member of the tonic triad of Song 4, and emerges as the root of the tonic triad in Song 5.]

7) All the features of category 6) are present, and in addition, a single key governs the entire work. In tonal instrumental works, we are quite accustomed to finding the outer movements in the same key, which then determines the range of possible keys for the inner movements—usually the same or diatonically related keys, such as VI, III, or IV. (Haydn's Piano Sonata in E♭ major is a rare exception; the second movement is in E♮ major.) But a quick glance at the wide range of keys of the sixteen *Dichterliebe* songs—there are nine keys, irrespective of modal changes—and in particular at the different keys of

1. *The Thematic Process in Music*, New York, 1951; *Thematic Patterns in the Sonatas of Beethoven*, New York, 1967.

the outer songs (A major and C♯ minor), will reveal the lack of an obvious single key controlling the entire work. It should be noted that a demonstration that *Dichterliebe* belongs to category 5) or even to category 6) would not necessarily imply the preeminence of a single key throughout the cycle. By way of example, Songs 1-5 constitute a coherent subsection of the cycle for reasons that I have intimated above; but while the coherence of this subsection depends upon the ordered set of keys of Songs 1-5, it does not follow that I regard any one note as the tonic of the five songs taken as a whole.

All the same, I do intend to present in the following pages an overall compositional plan according to which the sixteen songs of *Dichterliebe* are interdependent "movements" governed by a single key. There are two large parts, consisting respectively of Songs 1-7 and 8-16.[2] The first part consists of two subsections (Songs 1-5 and 6-7), the second part of three (Songs 8-12, 13-14, and 15-16).

The remaining portion of this essay is divided into three parts. In the. first, I shall describe Songs 1-5, both individually and with respect to their interrelationships as members of a unified subsection. In the second part, drawing upon the musical implications of Songs 1-5, I shall describe and attempt to justify the overall plan of the cycle. In the third part, I shall present descriptions of the remaining songs, 6-16.

I. THE BEGINNING OF THE CYCLE:
SONGS 1—5

1

Song 1 is justly famous for the ambiguity of its key. The opening four measures suggest F♯ minor, but no F♯ triad appears, either here or elsewhere in the song. With F♯ as overall tonic, the local tonic in mm. 5-8 would be interpreted as III; but the two authentic A major cadences coordinated with the entrance of the voice part in m. 5 instead project F♯ minor as VI. In either case, two related questions arise: if A is tonic, what explains the prominence of the F♯ minor scale at the extremes of each verse, and particularly at the end of the song? Conversely, if F♯ is tonic, why the absence of F♯ triads throughout the song?

The answer to these questions will emerge from a consideration of the structural relationships of the entire cycle, and I defer further discussion of the problem of key in Song 1 until Part II below. For now,

2. The unequal size of these two parts does not correspond to the original publication of the cycle in two volumes consisting of eight songs each, with a separate title page before Song 9.

I shall assume A major as tonic, and proceed to examine some other details of the song.

The four-measure piano introduction presents contrary-motion linear connections between D-C♯ and B-C♯; at the same time, the B of mm. 1 and 3 is retained as C♯ enters in mm. 2 and 4 (Ex. 4a). Thus, although B and D are resolved by C♯ at one structural level, B is present along with C♯ at a more background level (Ex. 4b).[3] In the fore-

Ex. 4   a)   b)

ground, one finds further references to these linear connections: observe the right-hand appoggiatura, D, mm. 2 and 4, and the added bass motion, B-C♯, in the piano interlude and postlude.

In the first phrase of the voice part, D is again an upper neighbor to C♯—resolving first in the piano part, then in the voice part at m.6— but B changes from a lower neighbor to a passing-note, proceeding to A. This inversion of the motion B-C♯ to B-A is reflected in the foreground figures B-G♯-F♯-E♯ (mm. 1-2), and D-F♯-G♯-A (mm. 5-6); the second figure inverts the intervallic content of the first while retaining the same metric-rhythmic pattern (Ex. 5).[4]

Ex. 5   a)   b)

3. The reader unfamiliar with the concept of structural level, and other basic concepts associated with Heinrich Schenker's theories, should consult Allen Forte, *Schenker's Conception of Musical Structure,* in *Journal of Music Theory,* III/1 (April 1959), 1-30, portions of which are reprinted below, pp. 96-106. Schenker's final work, *Der freie Satz,* Vienna, 1935; 2nd rev. ed., 1956, can be found in many libraries, but unfortunately an English translation is not readily available. Schenker's early *Harmonielehre* (1906) has been translated into English (under the title *Harmony,* Chicago, 1954), but many of Schenker's later concepts are not yet formulated in this early work. I should add that my own application of Schenker's theories is not entirely orthodox (assuming that *Der freie Satz* is accepted as a standard of orthodoxy).

4. The inversional relationship between these two four-note figures was pointed out to me by Prof. David Lewin of the State University of New York at Stony Brook.

Elements of vocal phrases 1 and 2 appear prominently in phrase 3 (mm. 9-10). The three notes, B, C♯, and D, are presented once again, this time in a passing motion; and the accompanying IV⁶–V⁷–I progression in B minor resembles the II⁶–V⁷–I of mm. 5-6. Moreover, the tonicization of B minor has been prepared by the arpeggiation B-D-F♯ in the voice part of m. 5. And finally, the suspended E of m. 10 is a transposition of the suspended D in the piano part of m. 6. (The E is not found in the composer's manuscript; Schumann added it later to the published version.) A curious detail is the extension of the right-hand B and C♯ in m. 9, allowing the piano B and voice C♯ to sound together at the second beat—reminiscent of the joint presence of B and C♯ in mm. 2 and 4. (Note that the piano C♯ and voice D are not correspondingly overlapped in m. 10.) The piano appoggiaturas of m. 10 recall the introductory appoggiaturas of m. 1.

Phrase 4, mm. 11-12, is sequentially modeled after phrase 3—a minor third higher. The tonicization of D major, like that of B minor, is prepared in the initial vocal phrase: the D of m. 5 remains unresolved in both the voice and piano parts at the cadence on A in m. 6, and the joint presence of D and A implies D as tonic. Indeed, in some respects phrase 4 bears a closer resemblance to phrases 1 and 2 than to phrase 3: the piano part in m. 12 is more an imitation (a fourth higher) of mm. 6 and 8 than of m. 10; and the fifth-descent, A-D, in mm. 11-12, compared to the fourth-ascent, F♯-B, in mm. 9-10, with the consequent association of the low bass notes A (mm. 6-8) and D (m. 12), suggests the background priority of D rather than B with respect to A (Ex. 6). As soon as the fourth phrase is completed, D is reinterpreted as the sixth scale degree of F♯ minor—with G♯-F♯ of the piano part replacing G♮-F♯ in the voice—and the repetitions proceed.

Ex. 6

Ex. 6 shows the large-scale harmonic progression of Song 1, A-D-C♯, with the B of mm. 9-10 resolving to A in the course of the bass motion from A to D. In the course of each verse, B appears first as a passing-note, then as a neighbor-note, and, as the piano solo starts, again as a neighbor-note. The neighbor B (next to middle C) in the interlude resolves to A at the beginning of verse 2, but the "same" B an octave higher is left unresolved at the end of verse 2. (Observe the voice-exchange between B and G♯ in the final measure, as compared to mm. 2, 4, etc.)

When the middleground D is omitted, the background shows an arpeggiation, C♯-A-C♯, in the bass part, with a concurrent linear motion, B-A-B under a pedal C♯ in the upper parts (Ex. 7). The background of Song 1 is unique in four ways: the triadic third, C♯, is retained in the upper part throughout, rather than being replaced by the principal linear note, B; B receives dissonant harmonic support (from C♯); B is accompanied by E♯, the chromatic neighbor to F♯; and the subsidiary linear chord (C♯⁷) occupies the external locations usually assigned to the tonic triad, while the latter is relegated to the middle position. (A typical *Ursatz*[5] in A major is illustrated in Ex. 8.)

Ex. 7   Ex. 8

I shall conclude the discussion of Song 1 with reference to one other interesting feature of the song: the relatively high frequency of suspensions and appoggiaturas. The initial unaccompanied upbeat, C♯, is suspended in m. 1, while that bar also contains the appoggiaturas A♯ and G♯. In mm. 2 and 4, D appears in the top part as an appoggiatura, while the bass D in mm. 1 and 3 is an appoggiatura with respect to C♯ in mm. 2 and 4. Like the bass D, F♯ in mm. 1 and 3 is a middleground appoggiatura with respect to E♯ in mm. 2 and 4; and in a higher octave, F♯ also functions as a foreground resolution of the appoggiatura G♯.

Similar examples of delay are found in the verses proper. The II⁶ chord in m. 5 is metrically accented with respect to its resolution, the V⁷ chord at beat 2; while in the middleground the V⁷ chord itself is correspondingly accented with respect to the I chord in m. 6 (Ex. 9). C♯ and

5. For a full discussion of this term see Allen Forte [*Schenker's Analysis of Song 2*], p. 96-106 below.

F♯ in the voice part of m. 5 delay B and G♯, respectively; and the accompaniment in m. 6 includes D both as a suspension at the first beat and as an appoggiatura during the second beat (prepared, as an implied suspension, in m. 5).

Ex. 9

More of the same linear-rhythmic relationships are found in the remainder of the song. The absence of a resolution for the final C♯⁷ chord—made more acute by virtue of the fermatas—represents another example of delay. C♯ is neither displaced by the B⁶ chord as in all its previous occurrences, nor resolved by an F♯ minor triad, as its V⁷ structure invites.

In Song 1, the prominence of linear connections entailing delay is significant for two reasons: 1) A fairly consistent emphasis on delay occurs throughout Songs 1-5, binding these songs into a single unit (in view of the virtual absence of delay in most of song 6). 2) A linear connection is brought into foreground focus when the first member—as a suspension or appoggiatura—delays the attack of the second member. The note B often delays its displacements in Song 1. Some of the B's resolve down to A, while others resolve up to C♯, and the final B remains unresolved until Song 2. Thus, Song 1 stresses linear displacements of the note B, leaving the direction of its final displacement undetermined.

I have made a point of discussing Song 1 in great detail in view of its germinal position at the inception of the cycle. To sum up, Song 1 is in the key of A but makes a point of hanging onto B. This suggests the remaining course of the cycle: to hang onto B and eventually resolve it to either A or C♯.

2

Song 2 is among the briefest of songs, but its apparent simplicity belies the perplexities of its structure. In recent years, the song has aroused an extraordinary amount of interest, much of which can be attributed to its selection as the principal illustration of Schenker's analytic technique in Allen Forte's important introductory article on Schenker's theories.[6]

The song is remarkable in several respects: 1) the note B is left unresolved in the voice part at the ends of phrases 1, 2, and 4;[7] 2) the middle of the song contains an unusual harmonic progression: E major-B minor-C♯ major-A major[7]-D major-A major; and 3) while the melodic "recapitulation" occurs at the beginning of phrase 4, the harmony at that point tonicizes D major, rather than A major.

The major analytic issue concerns G♮ at the beginning of the fourth phrase. According to the most obvious interpretation, G♮ passes from G♯ to F♯. But this raises a question about the relationship between C♯ and D in mm. 12-14. Considering the metrical and pitch relationships of just the outer parts, C♯ and D form a complete neighbor-note motion (Ex. 10), by analogy with the opening linear motions of phrases 1 and 2. Ex. 11 illustrates the conflict between the time-span embracing the passing

Ex. 10   Ex. 11

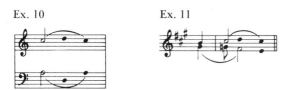

motion from G♯ to F♯ and the time-span in which the C♯-D neighbor-note motion occurs. However, if D is subsidiary to the first C♯, then C♯ and A should resolve B and G♯, respectively, from m. 12 (Ex. 12). But if G♯ is resolved by A, then how can G♮ pass from G♯ to F♯? (I do not share Forte's view that G♮ passes from A.) Conversely, if G♮ is inferior to F♯, then the entire A[7] chord should resolve to the D chord (Ex. 13), in which case C♯ emerges as a passing-note from B to D.

6. Cf. footnote 3, above.

7. Schenker cites these phrases in his discussion of the half-cadence in his *Harmonielehre* (1906). "The vocal part first brings the half-close, whereupon the piano follows immediately with the full close. The author most appropriately indicates the distinction between both kinds of closes by the position of the legato slur in the piano part. It is true that basically this example represents a perfect full close; by interrupting at the dominant, however, the vocal part succeeds, at least for the duration of the fermata, in most convincingly simulating the effect of a half-close." Cf. *Harmony*, ed. by Oswald Jonas. tr. by Elizabeth Mann Borgese. University of Chicago Press, 1954, p. 221. According to Viktor Ernst Wolff, the fermatas over B were added sometime after the song was originally composed. Cf. *Lieder Robert Schumanns in ersten und späteren Fassungen*, Leipzig, 1914, p. 82.

Ex. 12   Ex. 13

In his analytic sketches (p. 95, below), Schenker acknowledges the
G♮ but does not explain it. And in spite of the marked harmonic
difference between mm. 1 and 13, Schenker analyses the two passages
alike—D is, in each case, a neighbor to the two adjacent C♯'s. Forte
disagrees with Schenker, viewing the last phrase as essentially different
from the first, and places the return of the headnote, C♯, in m. 14 *after*—
rather than preceding—the tonicized D. I find both views compelling, and
have attempted to reconcile them in the following analysis.

The difficulty in regarding the C♯ in mm. 12-13 as a passing-note
from B is precisely that in the analogous passage in mm. 1-2, C♯ does
not appear to be subsidiary to D. But observe the following factors at
the beginning of the song: 1) the metrical position of D in m. 2 is much
stronger than the initial upbeat attack-point of the tied C♯; 2) the bass
line prolongs A-D-A, the triadic fifth of D major; 3) the harmonic
support for C♯ in m. 1 is weak compared to the complete A major triad
in m. 2; and 4) the A in m. 2 occupies a genuine bass register, while
in m. 1 A is like an inner voice. Therefore, in view of the B left hanging
at the end of Song 1, the initial C♯ of Song 2 can be regarded as a local
passing-note to the neighbor D, which resolves directly to C♯ in the same
measure. In keeping with this analysis, the opening and recapitulatory
foreground phrases remain equivalent in the middleground (Ex. 14).

Ex. 14

Of course, the evidence which suggested this analysis to me is the
remarkable return of B minor-C♯ major-A major from Song 1. For

the same progression occurs from the end of Song 1 into the opening of Song 2, as well as in mm. 11-13, Song 2. And there is logic in the change of harmonic support for B in the third phrase from E major (m. 9) to C♯ major; for of the three B-D ascents of Song 2, the first starts from the final C♯⁷ chord of Song 1, the second from the E⁷ chord in m. 4, and the third from the third phrase, mm. 9-12, which includes both E and C♯ in support of B.

The conjunction of G♮ and the A major triad provides the rationale for viewing C♯ as a passing-note in mm. 12-13. Observe the voice part ornament, C♯-B-C♯, which affirms this view by placing the last C♯ of m. 13 between B and D. Another affirmation is found in the G♮ in m. 10, which passes (under C♯) to F♯ in m. 11, preparing us to interpret the second G♮ in like fashion.

Finally, the end of the song leaves B unresolved in the voice part, just as Song 1 leaves B unresolved in the piano part. So while Song 2 supplies a resolution (C♯) for the unresolved B of Song 1, it also leaves B very much in evidence at the end of the song. The function of Song 2 in the cycle is generally to strengthen the harmonic support for B while clarifying the key of Song 1. A major is not in doubt as tonic of Song 2, and the associations between the two songs—we should not overlook the fact that in neither song does a C♯⁷ chord ever resolve to an F♯ minor triad—forges them virtually into a single entity.

3

The hanging B at the end of the voice part of Song 2 resolves vocally in the upbeat A of Song 3. The weakening of A from tonic to dominant status coincides with the upgrading of B from a dissonance to a consonance with respect to the prevailing tonic note, D. Numerous associations connect Songs 1 and 2 with Song 3: the use of the same four pitches at the start of the vocal line, the explicit treatment of C♯ as descending passing-note between D and B,[8] as well as in the now familiar reverse direction; and the use of B as appoggiatura at the end of the vocal part. The last three notes of the vocal part—B-A-D—reiterate the connection in the voice part between Songs 2 and 3, with B delaying A in each case. Indeed, as I have indicated in the analytic sketch in Ex. 15, B is prominent in the middleground throughout most of the song. (The

8. Schenker regards the C♯ of Song 2. m. 2, as a passing-note with consonant support. Without sharing this view, I acknowledge the linear association of these three notes—due to directional changes in the melody.

Ex. 15

L (Rep.)

reader should also consult the analytic sketches by Schenker, pp. 107-08
below.)

Song 3 is also noteworthy for certain elements that appear for the
first time in the cycle. The interval D-B is supported for the first time
in a G major harmony—in mm. 1-3, 5-7, 12, and 17-21. And C♮ is used
as a passing-note between D and B for the first time (m. 12). Moreover,
the tonicizations of Song 3 reflect the key directions both before and
after Song 3: I am referring to the sequential progression that starts
in A major in m. 9, proceeds to D major in m. 10, and arrives at G major
in m. 12.

4

In view of the preceding discussion, the prominence of B and D
at the beginning of Song 4 requires no comment. For the first time, B
is presented as a member of the prevailing tonic triad.

The subdominant tendencies of the preceding songs are exceeded
here, inasmuch as the IV—C major—is approached via its own IV, F
major. While C major is not the key of the next song, the tonicizations
in the middle of Song 4—C major, E minor, and A minor—do anticipate
the keys of Songs 6, 7, and 8 (not in that order). And the first three
songs are recalled by the prominent suspended B in m. 14.

The principal linear motion of the song is the displacement of
B by its upper neighbor, C, in m. 8. The semi-sequential approaches to
C in mm. 6-8 and to G in mm. 14-16 suggest a background top-part skip,
C-G. The coda then resolves the hanging C, supported once again in a C
major triad.

Ex. 16 contains an analytic sketch of the song; the reader should
also consult Schenker's analysis, p. 109, below. The principal difference
between the two sketches hinges on the analysis of B in m. 14. Schenker
regards it as a return to the headnote, $\hat{3}$, whereas I consider it a suspen-

Ex. 16

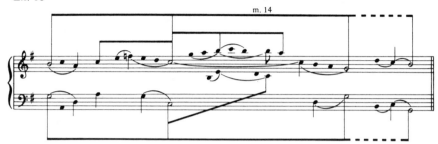

sion of the middleground connection between C and A—which anticipates the return of A as (minor) tonic of Song 8. In this regard, notice the
association of C-B-A in the right-hand piano octaves, mm. 10-14.

The large-scale sequential relationships between IV and I suggest
the superiority of the principal voice notes C-D over the optional notes
G-F♮, in m. 7: the C and D correspond to the G and A at the first beat
of m. 15. (The optional notes are not found in the composer's manuscript
of 1840.) The missing corresponding $\hat{5}$-$\hat{4}$-$\hat{3}$ line in the piano part of
m. 15—cf. ʹG-F♮-E in the piano part of m. 7—turns up in the coda,
the function of the delay being to resolve the upper neighbor C down to
B.

5

The progressive increase in harmonic support for B now reaches its
acme as B becomes the root of the tonic triad of Song 5.

In the initial bars of Song 5, we again encounter what might be
labeled the *Ur-incipit*: the arpeggiation of B-D in linear association with
C♯. And the parallelisms between Songs 1 and 5 are particularly striking: 1) the opening upbeat of Song 5 resembles the upbeat C♯ of Song
1—each is literally unsupported by other notes, is suspended into the
following measure, and is the main note of the initial harmonic progression; 2) each song contains a melodic sequence of the scale-degrees
$\hat{1}$-$\hat{2}$-$\hat{3}$, first in B minor, then in D major, supported in nearly identical
harmonic progressions—the IV[6] chords of Song 1, mm. 9 and 11, being
included within the II[7] chords of Song 5, mm 1 and 5, respectively. Moreover, the vocal appoggiaturas E and G♮ of Song 1, mm. 10 and 12, are
represented respectively in the linear motions E-D and G-F♯ in the piano
part of Song 5, mm. 1-2 and 5-6.

In connection with the progressively increasing support for B throughout Songs 1-5, it should be noted that in the melody, D precedes B at the beginnings of Songs 2 and 3, whereas B precedes D in Songs 4 and 5. In Song 1, the D major sequence in mm. 11-12 is structurally superior to the B minor prolongation in mm. 9-10, due to the lower register of D (in the bass) and the similarity of the piano figuration of m. 12 to the A major figuration in mm. 6 and 8. But in Song 5, the D major sequence is clearly inferior to the B minor prolongation—witness the repetition of the latter in mm. 3-4, the presence of the dissonance, C♯, in conjunction with the D major triad in m. 6, and the placement of the G⁷ chord instead of a D⁶ chord in the same measure.

The coda of Song 5 is the first of several extensive piano postludes to be found in *Dichterliebe*. The content of the postlude recalls earlier songs and anticipates Song 6, as well as referring to elements in Song 5 proper. The B minor-C♯ major harmonic progression of Songs 1-2 is found in m. 18; and here again the E♯ is displaced by E♮. The top-line motion C-B-A-G in mm. 17-18 appears in the melody of Song 6, mm. 4-6, and the tonic triad of Song 6, E minor, occurs several times throughout the postlude. The bass motion B-D-C♯-B-A♯ that starts the postlude, reverses the voice motion, A♯-B-C♯-D-B of mm. 1-2; E-D-C-A♯-B in mm. 19-20 repeats the top part of mm. 15-16; and the inner-part motions G-E-F♯ and E-C♯-D, in the final three measures, recall the top-part lines in the piano part, mm. 5-6 and 1-2, respectively.

To summarize my reasons for regarding Songs 1-5 as a unit:

B is initially presented as a dissonant seventh in a C♯ major chord, and forms a major second with the tonic, A, of Song 1. In Song 2, B still forms a major second with the tonic, but mainly receives consonant support in E major triads. In Song 3, B forms a consonance with the tonic D, but remains outside the tonic triad. In Song 4, B is a triadic third, and becomes the tonic in Song 5. (This process is reversed in Song 6, where B becomes the V prior to its displacement by C♮ in Song 7.)

Delay is a prominent feature at various structural levels throughout the five songs. All the songs start in the same vocal register, emphasizing the notes B, D, and C♯ (C♮ in Song 4). All the songs are relatively soft. And, finally, almost the entire content of Song 5 is found in Song 1. These remarks take on added weight in view of the notable absence of these features from Song 6.

The marked interdependence of Songs 1-5 provides an answer to the biographical question concerning Schumann's omission of Songs 4a and 4b from the first published edition of *Dichterliebe*. While certain elements in these two songs match elements in other songs of the cycle, neither of them particularly resembles Songs 1-5, and their keys (E♭ major and G minor) interfere with the process that culminates in the arrival at B minor as tonic of Song 5.

II. THE OVERALL FORM OF THE CYCLE

The overall form of *Dichterliebe* can be viewed as an outgrowth of the initial tonal events of the cycle. As tonic of Song 1, A is the principal note at the beginning of the cycle, yet B and C♯ impinge on the primacy of A at the beginning, middle and end of that song. In fact, the C♯⁷ chord raises doubt about the key of the first song, and it is only the clarity of A major in Song 2, along with numerous similarities between Songs 1 and 2, which relieves that doubt. As the only pair of adjacent songs in the same key, Songs 1 and 2 make a strong case for hypothesizing A major as the key of the cycle. The incomplete linear motion A-B of Song 1 (cf. Ex. 7) is completed with the resolution of B to C♯ at the outset of Song 2. Songs 1-5 represent a still larger unit in which A also moves to B, as in the incomplete linear motion of Song 1. The key of B minor gives way to various other keys after Song 5, but B returns as tonic (in the major mode) in Song 14, followed by C♯ minor at the end of the cycle. I propose an overall view according to which the arpeggiated interval A-C♯ is filled in by the passing-note B, with an interruption in the motion from B to C♯ between Songs 5 and 14 (see Ex. 17).

Ex. 17

In order to make sense of the content of the cycle between Songs 5 and 14, it will be necessary to focus on two main elements, which I shall label the *harmonic plan* and the *modal plan*. Observe the key progressions in Songs 1-5, which demonstrate both the harmonic plan and the modal plan. The harmonic plan involves treating a given note in successive songs first as tonic, then as dominant; it is then displaced in the next song by an ascending scale-step as the sixth scale-degree (6̂) of its subdominant, which simultaneously or eventually becomes the new tonic. Thus, in Ex. 17a, the note A (the tonic of Songs 1 and 2) is replaced by D as the tonic of Song 3, after which A is displaced by B in Song 4, and B becomes the tonic in Song 5. The modal plan involves retaining the given modes of the diatonic scale degrees involved in the harmonic plan—in other words, avoiding modal mixture. Thus, A major is followed by D major, not D minor, and D major is followed by G *major* which is followed by B *minor*. The harmonic and modal plans essentially control the remaining course of the cycle.

Ex. 17a

As the second main note of the cycle, B is treated like A, in accordance with both the harmonic and modal plans (Ex. 17b): in Song 6 B becomes the dominant of E minor and is then displaced in Song 7 by C♮, which is both 6 of E minor and the tonic (in the major mode) of Song 7. The motion of B to C♮ in Song 7 is analogous to a deceptive cadence in the overall motion A-B-C♯. Song 8, in the key of A minor, represents the onset of a second effort to breach the interval A-C♯ with the passing-note B.

Ex. 17b

The content of the seven songs from Song 8 to Song 14 bears a strong resemblance to the content of the first seven. Songs 8-12 provide increasingly strong support for B♭, closely paralleling the treatment of B♮ in Songs 1-5: B♭ is emphasized as a chromatic neighbor throughout Song 8 (forming a dissonant interval with A); in Song 9, B♭ forms a consonant interval with respect to the new tonic, D, and is particularly prominent in the tonicizations of G minor in the second and fourth parts; B♭ emerges as the third of G minor in Song 10, as the fifth of E♭ major in Song 11, and finally as the root of B♭ major in Song 12. The harmonic and modal plans both apply to the key progressions from Song 8 to Song 12 (Ex. 17c); A becomes $\frac{6}{5}$ of D minor, after which A is displaced by B♭, the $\overset{\wedge}{6}$ of D minor. The descending-fifth motions in Songs 2-3-4 are repeated in Songs 8-9-10, and only E♭ major in Song 11 digresses from the scheme of key progressions exhibited in Songs 1-5.

Ex. 17c

The single digression from the modal plan in the entire cycle occurs at Song 13. In conjunction with the continued application of the harmonic plan to essential notes, B♭ is displaced in Song 14 by C♭, the $\overset{\wedge}{6}$ of E♭ *minor* (Ex. 17d), rather than by C♮, the $\overset{\wedge}{6}$ of E♭ *major*. The occurrence of modal mixture in Song 13 is prepared in Song 11 (in E♭ major) by the presence of G♭ major, and in Song 12, mm. 8-9, by the enharmonic exploitation of the G♭ augmented-sixth chord as V⁷ of C♭ major (which is VI of E♭ *minor*).

Ex. 17d

C♭ is the enharmonic equivalent of B♮, and both the harmonic and modal plans are adhered to as B major in Song 14 gives way to E major in Song 15 and to C♯ minor in Song 16 (Ex. 17e). The avoidance of C♮ minor in Song 14 (effected by the modal change to E♭ minor in Song 13) not only reinstates B♮, but also avoids arriving at C♯ (D♭) in the major mode (through the application of the harmonic and modal plans in Songs 14-16—C minor, F minor, D♭ major). Thus, although no song in A occurs near the end of the cycle, the scale of A major nevertheless controls the final events of the cycle: the modal switch to E♭ minor in Song 13 effects the return of B♮ and the arrival at C♯ minor as the modally correct III of A major.

Ex. 17e

In summary, Part I exhibits the motion A-B-C♮, and subdivides into two subsections (Songs 1-5 and 6-7) embracing one ascending stepwise motion each. Part II consists of two complete stepwise motions, the one (A-B♭-C♭) nested within the other (A-B♮-C♯), with three subsections (Songs 8-12, 13-14, and 15-16) embracing one ascending stepwise motion each (Ex. 18). The motion to B♭ major in Part II follows from the combination of the harmonic and modal plans (applied to A minor); the extension of Part II by two extra songs, in conjunction with the breach in the modal plan at Song 13, involves the "correction" of the passing-note B♭ to B♮, and the ultimate conclusion of the cycle on C♯.

Ex. 18

In tonal pieces, the final chord is usually I; in *Dichterliebe* it is III. The stability of C♯ (III) is shored up by the presence of D♯ (E♭) in Songs 11 and 13-16, and the change to C♯ (D♭) major in the postlude of Song 16. The presence there of E♯ tends to deny locally the structural priority of A major, since E♯ is chromatic with respect to A. But there is no actual doubt about the subsidiary relationship of C♯ to A, in view of the large-scale arpeggiation of A-C♯, the absence of G♯ as a song key, and the final approach to the key of C♯ from B♮ (as I of Song 14 and V of Song 15), rather than from B♯.

The treatment of C♯ as a quasi-tonic at the end of *Dichterliebe* recalls the significant placement of C♯ at the end of Song 1. In addition, the E♯ in Song 1 can be understood in the same light as the E♯ (F♮) in the postlude of Song 16—it stabilizes C♯. Considering the association of the C♯ major triad with the notes B and D, the implication of F♯ minor in Song 1 is unavoidable; but in the context of the entire cycle, it turns out to be minimal—since, after all, the only resolution of a root-position C♯⁷ chord by an F♯ minor triad occurs in m. 24 of Song 16, where F♯ is explicitly established at the outset as IV of C♯. So, the tritone, E♯-B, of Song 1 represents not one, but two different scales: C♯ major and A major. The final measure of Song 1 makes C♯ particularly explicit as a local tonic, since as a consequence of the G♯-B voice exchange (cf. mm. 2, 4, etc.), only members of the C♯ major triad are attacked during the first beat.

The necessity for considering the final outcome of the cycle in order to clarify the initial E♯ signifies the magnitude of the extent to which the songs of *Dichterliebe* constitute parts of a whole. And the coherence of the whole explains Schumann's omission of Songs 4a and 4b and 12a and 12b. As I have already said, Songs 4a and 4b interfere with the progressive increase in support of B♮ in Songs 1-5. And Songs 12a and 12b —in the keys of G minor and B♭ major—tend to overstress B♭ and unsuitably delay the stepwise ascent from B♭ to C♭-B♮ to C♯. In the absence of Songs 12a and 12b, the stepwise progression from B♭ to C♯ occurs in the minimum number of songs (four) in accordance with the harmonic plan. The cohesiveness of this progression is underscored by the association between the postludes of Songs 12 and 16.[9]

III. THE REMAINDER OF THE CYCLE: SONGS 6—16

6

I have already suggested that Song 6 differs in several ways from Songs 1-5; it is relatively loud, begins in a low vocal range, and has few suspensions and appoggiaturas. Also, it does not share the motivic-harmonic interrelationships of Songs 1-5, and it reverses the progressive increase in support for the pitch-class B that occurs in those songs. But I think the most remarkable individual quality of Song 6 is the contrapuntal independence of the piano part. This is not to imply that there is no contrapuntal interest in the piano parts of Songs 1-5; but with respect to this factor they do not evoke special comment. In Song 6, on the other hand, the initial vocal melody merely doubles the bass, while the genuine top part lies in the two-note eighth-dotted-quarter rhythmic figures of the piano part. This figure is eventually taken up by the voice, starting with the upbeat to m. 19, but the piano part never gives it up and makes much of it long after the completion of the voice part in m. 42. Note the left-hand accompaniment figure, mm. 17-19 (Ex. 19a), and its varied repetition in the piano interlude starting in m. 27 (Ex. 19b) , and in the voice phrase starting in m. 31 (Ex. 19c) .

In spite of the differences between Song 6 and Songs 1-5, there are some elements which unite them. Aside from the postlude of Song 5 (cf.

9. Cf. pp. 92-93 for further discussion of this equivalence.

Ex. 19a

Ex. 19b

Ex. 19c

p. 76 above), the main anticipation of Song 6 exists in Song 4; the key of Song 6 is E minor and its principal tonicizations are A minor and G major, while the key of Song 4 is G major and among its principal tonicizations are A minor and E minor.

In the final vocal phrase, starting at the end of m. 35, the voice imitates the piano—but the voice has skips, like the right-hand part at the beginning of the song, while the piano includes steps, which typify the voice part up to this point. The postlude varies the opening of the song, by extending the C-E descent (mm. 4-7) down to A—anticipating the long descending bass lines of Song 7.

7

The key of Song 7 has been anticipated in Song 4 by the broad tonicization of C major, within which the melodic figures E-D-C-F—at the opening of Song 7—and F-E-D-C—near its end—are both present. The bass motion, A-B-C, of Song 6 (mm. 35-40), is found in mm. 13-19 of Song 7, and the C-B-A-G line of Song 6 (mm. 4-7) constitutes most of the last vocal phrase of Song 7.

Song 7 is one of the most famous songs in the lied repertory. One of its special characteristics is the succession of overlapping seventh chords in mm. 5-9 and 23-29. Observe that the B of m. 5 is resolved by A in m. 6, while E remains as a seventh over F. As the bass F moves to E in the same measure, G is introduced, forming an inverted seventh with A. As the G is resolved by F in m. 7, C remains over the bass D, and so forth. In his harmony book, Schoenberg raised the question whether the sevenths originate as linear connections or as suspensions, and suggested that the answer is uncertain.[10] In my view, none of the sevenths

10. Arnold Schoenberg, *Harmonielehre*, 3rd ed., Vienna, 1922, p. 407.

are suspensions; rather, they arise due to the combination of foreground passing-notes and middleground chord notes (pedals). (See Ex. 20.)

Ex. 20

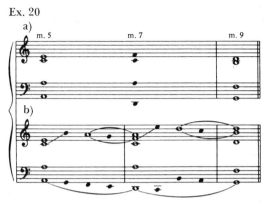

The second verse is noteworthy for the extension of the sequence of mm. 5-8 into six measures, with the piano reaching A^2 and the voice beginning an optional linear descent from A^2 as well. I think that Schumann made the right decision in offering these climactic notes to the singer (as well as to the pianist), and I assume that he retained the original voice notes only out of concern for singers of limited vocal range.[11]

The dynamic nature of Song 7 suggests regarding it as the final member of a large-scale unit, in which the emphasized B of the preceding songs is firmly resolved by C. At the same time, the several linear connections between G and A in the last five bars anticipate the continuation of the cycle in Song 8 in the key of A minor.

8

The initial motive of Song 7 (E-D-C-F) is represented in Song 8 by E-D-C in m. 1 and the climactic F in mm. 2-3. Song 8 also relates back to Songs 1-2, insofar as A is again the tonic, albeit in the minor mode. As in Songs 1-2, a note located a scale-step above the tonic appears prominently throughout Song 8. In this case, however, the note in question, B♭, chromatically replaces the highly emphasized B♮ of Songs 1-2. Occurring first in the Neapolitan harmony of mm. 3-4, B♭ represents 6̂ in the D

11. Grieg mistakenly believed that Schumann added the lower notes as optional for the singer (cf. p. 120 below). In fact, the higher notes are not present in the composer's manuscript, and appear for the first time in the original published edition (1844).

minor scale, rather than $\hat{2}$ in the A minor scale, and anticipates the tonicization of D minor in verse 4 (starting at m. 24) as well as the key of D
minor in Song 9. The prominence of B♭ also signals the onset of the general upgrading of this note in this part of the cycle, culminating in its
appearance as tonic in Song 12.

The fourth verse differs in several respects from the first three
strophic verses. The sequential ascent of the second phrase is replaced
by a stepwise descent; and a literal transposition of the A⁷ chord in m. 25
is avoided in favor of a G minor 7th chord—bringing in B♭ again. The
effect of the descending sequence is to outline the foreground E-D-C of the
opening phrase of the song in the top part of the middleground motion
embracing the first five measures (25-29) of the fourth verse (Ex. 21).

Ex. 21

The last two phrases of the fourth verse loosely resemble the last two
phrases of verses 1-3, with the peculiar introduction of B♮ in phrase 3
before B♭ in phrase 4, rather than the other way around. Thus, as the
voice part ends, A is presented as the V of D minor (which includes B♭
in its scale), rather than as tonic (which includes B♮); and this harmonic
implication is picked up in the postlude as well. Indeed, the left-hand
A-G-F-E in the postlude represents an almost complete transposition of
the initial melodic fifth descent of the song into the key of D minor.

9

The contrapuntal independence of Song 6 is found to an even
greater extent in Song 9; the piano has the tune, to which the voice
merely provides a rather square counterpoint. Another retrospective element is that the entire passage from m. 8 to m. 12 repeats the harmonic
progression of mm. 24-29 from the immediately preceding song.

The first verse-half proceeds to the mediant, F; while the second
verse-half—essentially a transposition of the first verse down a fifth, the
voice alterations being attributable mainly to range limitations—ends
on B♭. Thus, B♭ continues to receive emphasis, as in the preceding song;

and the association of B♭ with G♯ and A found in mm. 31-32 of Song 8 is repeated in mm. 32-34 of Song 9.

The coda begins with the dominant prolongation of mm. 1-4, followed directly by the V of G minor, as prolonged in mm. 17-20—bringing D and G into direct harmonic contact, in anticipation of G minor as the key of Song 10. The D major ending is not a genuine example of a modal alteration from minor to major; rather, the song ends on the V of IV (G minor), as a link to Song 10. However, the omission of E♭ in the final chromatic descent does stabilize D as I. The penultimate bar is notable for Schumann's notation of E♯ instead of F♮ in a piece in the key of D minor.

10

The arpeggiations in the piano part may be attributed to the text of the poem—representing a strumming accompaniment to the *Liedchen*—but the figuration is exploited for entirely musical purposes in the postlude. The final five notes of the voice part overlap the first three notes of the melody (B♭-A-G), a connection reinforced by the return of the theme in the higher register of the piano on the second sixteenth note of every beat—as in mm. 1-4. In m. 21, another overlap begins—one not exploited in m. 3—on off-beat eighth notes, while the theme continues on the second sixteenth note of each beat. Still another overlap begins in m. 23, with the new incipit taking over the eighth-note position as the continuation of the theme is put back to the second sixteenth note again. The culmination of this technique occurs in m. 24, with the lower G attacked *sforzando* on the second eighth note, and the higher G delayed until the fourth sixteenth note.

The postlude ends with long prolongations of the I$^6_4$ and I$^5_3$ chords that take their figurations from Song 9, mm. 17-19. Note the contraction of C and B♭ in m. 27, unlike the successive attacks of these notes in both mm. 26 and 29. The effect of the contraction is to reiterate the combination of the $\hat3$-$\hat2$-$\hat1$, $\hat5$-$\hat4$-$\hat3$, and $\hat5$-$\hat7$-$\hat8$ motives (mm. 21–22) at the final V-I progression (Ex. 22).

Ex. 22

Other interesting details:

The overall top-line motion of the song ($\hat{3}$-$\hat{4}$-$\hat{3}$-$\hat{2}$-$\hat{1}$) bears a superficial resemblance to that of the other song of the cycle with G as tonic (Song 4). The $\hat{5}$-$\hat{7}$-$\hat{8}$ motive of m. 7 is presented in the voice part as counterpoint to $\hat{3}$-$\hat{2}$-$\hat{1}$ in the C minor prolongation starting in m. 9. D♭ appears instead of D♮ in m. 10, effecting a somewhat less secure tonicization of C than the original prolongation of G—inasmuch as the prior phrase contains only notes which are diatonic with respect to G.

The text is supported in several places by musical elements in addition to the accompanimental strumming. The D♭ of m. 10 is associated with the words "wildem Schmerzendrang." Note also the thirty-second note figure for "auf" in m. 17, and the association of the high piano register with the adjective "übergrosses" in m. 19.

11

The figure B♭-E♭-D which ends the first voice phrase (mm. 7-8) is answered by B♭-D-E♭ at the end of the voice part (mm. 30-32). This follows a tonicization of G♭—the first of several in the next few songs—involving the resolution of C♭ to B♭ in the piano part, mm. 29-31. The linear relationship between C♭ and B♭ stands out prominently in Songs 12-14; in Song 14, the structural relationship of the two notes is reversed and C♭ (B♮) emerges as the resolution of B♭ (A♯). The G minor tonicization in mm. 21-22 refers back to the key of the preceding song. The coda reiterates the middleground top-line motion of the first verse (B♭ in mm. 1-8, C♮ in mm. 9-11, and B♭ in mm. 11-12), as well as the B♭-D-E♭ ending of the voice part.

12

G♭ is used initially in Song 12 as the bass of a German 6th chord in the key of B♭ major. But later, in m. 8, the same chord is enharmonically reinterpreted as the V⁷ of C♭ (B♮) major. Thus, in the very song in which B♭ is most stably prolonged—i.e., as tonic—it appears locally as the leading-tone of C♭, anticipating the future course of the cycle. However, the tonicization of C♭ is very weak by virtue of the seventh, A♮ (B♭♭) presented along with C♭, and B♭ is promptly retonicized in the next two measures. B♮ is presented in a different way—as the modally altered third of G minor (VI) —in the second verse, recalling the B-D arpeggiation of Song 4.

A curious rhythmic detail occurs in m. 11. Except for the last eight

measures, each measure contains two groups of five sixteenth notes. The
first note of each group is held as a quarter note, with just one exception:
m. 11, where the second sixteenth note, B♮, is held. The retention of B♮
supports the voice's cadential B♮, while the rhythmic placement of D
provides a resolution for the preceding E♭ at an appropriate attack-point
(the second sixteenth note).

The coda is of particular interest for three reasons: 1) like the coda
of Song 11, it emphasizes C being displaced by B♭ (Ex. 23) in addition to reiterating the B♭ major interpretation of the G♭ augmented sixth
chord (cf. mm. 9-10); 2) the resolutions of the augmented sixth chords
(in mm. 24 and 26) are irregular, compared to the conventional I$^6_4$
resolutions in mm. 2, 7, and 12, or the direct approach to V in m. 20;
and 3) mm. 23-28 are transposed up a minor third as the first part of the
coda of Song 16 (cf. pp. 92-93, below).

Ex. 23

13

The first two verses of Song 13 are noteworthy for the separate
articulations of voice and piano, as well as the silences between them.
By way of contrast, the piano and voice are heard jointly throughout
verse 3, which the piano introduces with the opening two-measure unaccompanied vocal motive in a I-IV-I harmonic setting. The initial
absence of piano support for the voice may be associated with the
pessimistic content of the first two verses, while the coordinated performance of new material is associated with the initial optimism of verse
3. The disappointment expressed in the last two lines of the verse is
reflected both in the chromatic support for the final tonic E♭ in the
voice part, m. 32, and in the recapitulatory piano motions starting in
m. 35.

The presence of G♭ in Songs 11 and 12 is fully exploited in Song 13—
first of all by virtue of its membership in the prevailing tonic triad, E♭
minor. The repeated D♭s of the G♭ major V-I progression of Song 11
are even more prominent in the third verse of Song 13, mm. 28-31.

Notice the hemiola rhythms in conjunction with the chromatic prolongation of the G♭ major triad in mm. 29-30. The three chromatic lines
here start at successive half-bar time-points, due to the different sizes
of the three intervals—D♭-G♭, B♭-D♭, and G♭-B♭ (proceeding from top
to bottom). Just as VI gives way to IV⁶ in verses 1 and 2 due to the
vocal motion G♭-G♮-A♭, III (G♭) gives way to IV in verse 3 via the
same chromatic passing-note, G♮ (cf. Exx. 24 and 25).

Ex. 24

VI   IV⁶

Ex. 25

III   IV

The linear connection B♭-C♭, to which I have called attention in
Songs 11 and 12, is further developed in Song 13. Aside from the opening
motive, it occurs in the middleground of all three verses (cf. Exx. 24
and 25). The support for C♭ in Song 13 is altogether more extensive
than in the preceding songs—anticipating the motion to the key of B♮
(C♭) major in Song 14.

The opening motive of Song 13 is a transposition down a minor
third from the opening two measures of the voice part of Song 2—cf.
Ex. 1. The level of transposition can be explained as follows: in Song
2, the C♯-D line anticipates the key of D in Song 3; in Song 13, the B♭-
C♭ line anticipates the key of B (C♭) in Song 14. Moreover, according to
the harmonic plan, the initial ascending motion from A major to B minor
(in Songs 1-5) includes an intermediary motion to the key of D major
(in Song 3). Now, late in the cycle, we find associations between the
early manifestation of the key of D and the subsequent return of B
as tonic of Song 14. Observe a similar association at the same transposi-

tion level between F♯-B-A-D which ends the voice part of Song 3 and
D♯-G♯-F♯-B which ends the interludes of Song 14.

Another association between the beginning of the cycle and Song
13 is found in the chromatic ascent from G♭, mm. 7-9 and 18-20, with
the appoggiatura B♭ leading to an A♭ minor sixth-chord—a downward
half-step transposition of a similar configuration in Song 4 (cf. Ex. 2).
The logic of the half-step transposition is based on the half-step interval
between the two heavily emphasized notes of Parts I and II of the cycle—
B♮ and B♭, respectively. The two passages are also related verbally: observe the presence of the words "weinen bitterlich" from the end of
Song 4 in the last two lines of verse 2 of song 13.

14

Song 14 begins with a reversal of the dependency relationship
between B♭ and C♭, now notated as A♯ and B♮. The sub-mediant key
relation from E♭ minor to B (C♭) major was prepared by the C♭ major
prolongations in Song 13, mm. 5-7 and 16-18. The two songs in the key
of B are associated by the repetition of the syncopated figure F♯-E♮-D♯
(in the bass part of Song 5, m. 8) in Song 14, m. 4 (Ex. 26).

Ex. 26   a) Song 5, m. 8   b) Song 14, m. 4

Verse 3 begins as a strophic repetition of verses 1 and 2, but the repetition extends only through the first two lines of the text. In the variant,
starting at m. 35, the G♯ minor triad is tonicized in the piano part and
prolonged in the voice part, realizing the implied tonicization of G♯—
due to Fx—in mm. 9 and 22.

It should be noted that many of the linear motions of this song
involve B and C♯, preparing the eventual large-scale ascent from B to
C♯ in Songs 14-16.

15

The length of Song 15 differentiates it from most of the other songs
of *Dichterliebe*. Its eight verses[12] are set in a non-strophic form that seems

12. Heine reduced the poem to six verses in later editions of the *Lyrisches
Intermezzo*.

more characteristic of instrumental pieces than of songs—an alternation of three themes in various keys, tantamount to a mixture of rondo and development, in which the first theme represents the refrain and the other two themes the intervening episodes. Theme 2, resembling the vocal line of Song 14, m. 10, appears in mm. 16-24, followed by the return of theme 1 in G major. Theme 3 enters at the upbeat of m. 29, first in G major, then sequentially in B major (mm. 32-36).

At this point, the piano repeats the first theme in I, but in a chromatic harmonic setting that anticipates the presentation of both themes 1 and 2 in V, starting at the upbeat of m. 41. At first the voice merely provides a kind of harmonic counterpoint—including the outline of theme 2 —but it resumes its thematic role in m. 45. At m. 56, we encounter a sequential episode which traverses the keys of the first four notes of theme 1: B, C♯, D♯, and E (emphasizing dominants, rather than their tonic resolutions).

An augmented recapitulation of the first theme begins with the upbeat to m. 69. (The augmentation provides the first interruption in the persistent reiteration of the eighth-quarter rhythmic figure.) Only the first portion of the theme is presented, however, after which theme 3, maintaining the augmentation, appears sequentially in I and IV, mm. 84-96. After a closing phrase in the voice part, the piano completes the song with a rhythmically altered version of the introduction.

In the overall harmonic-modal plan of the cycle, Song 15 (in E major) occupies a position analogous to that of Song 3 (in D major) — each representing the submediant precursor of the final song of a section (cf. Exx. 17a and e). This relationship is underscored by the similarity between a thematic segment of Song 3 and theme 3 of Song 15 (Ex. 27). Even more significant is the fact that the entire melody of

Ex. 27

a) Song 15, mm. 28-30   b) Song 3, mm. 11-12

Song 3 is represented by the augmented melody of Song 15—cf. Ex. 28, a transposition to E major of the main thematic notes of Song 3, in which the stemmed notes represent virtually all of the notes in mm. 68-104, Song 15. This whole-step transposition reflects the intervallic difference between the key groups at the beginning and ending of the cycle, again as shown in Exx. 17a and e.

Ex. 28

The end of Song 15 and the beginning of Song 16 interlock by virtue of the arpeggiation of the C♯ minor triad (Ex. 29). The function of the postlude of Song 15 is evidently not merely to recapitulate the introduction, but also—*vide* the repeated final I chord—to provide a final prominent G♯ to link with C♯ in Song 16.

Ex. 29

16

The quasi-tonic function of C♯ as the closing key of the cycle is established by numerous powerful prolongations of the tonic triad in Song 16. The piano introduces the song with an accented and sustained root-position C♯ minor triad, the range of which extends over most of the keyboard; this is followed by a fortissimo arpeggiation, I-V-I, which is repeated by the initial vocal entry. The harmony of the entire first verse (mm. 3-11) is limited to I, IV, and V, and only diatonic keys—III, IV, and V—are tonicized in the sequence (mm. 16-35) that fills out the main part of the song (ending in m. 43).[13] Even the voice part consists of mainly diatonic harmonic skips, especially in the recapitulatory fifth verse, starting in m. 36 and culminating with the parallel octaves (V-I) in mm. 42-43.

The final vocal skips of verse 5 (m. 40-43) presumably illustrate the notion of the huge coffin being dropped into the sea. The coffin's extra contents, which are hinted at in verse 2, are specified in verse 6:

13. Schumann apparently considered a chromatic modulation at m. 23. In a marginal note in the manuscript, he asks "oder nach f zu modulieren?" ("or modulate to F?").

the poet's love and sorrows. At this point, m. 44, the music recalls the
tonal material and soft dynamics of Songs 1 and 2, in which the poet's
love is first described. First, the tonic C♯ becomes the root of a seventh
chord, ornamented with the neighbor, D♮, reminiscent of the piano solos
of Song 1. Then, in mm. 47-49, the C♯⁷ chord moves to A⁷ and D major
chords, as in mm. 12-14 of Song 2, and the melody includes the lower
neighbor, B, of Song 2, m. 13 and the appoggiatura, E, of Song 1, m. 10.
Finally, C♯ is retonicized as D♮ gives way to D♯, while E♯ (F♮) remains
throughout the rest of the song. (Schumann originally notated the
postlude in C♯, but added a marginal note calling for the passage to be
engraved in D♭. The enharmonic renotation has no structural significance and was merely intended as a convenience for the reader.)

In the first part of the postlude, mm. 53-58, four of the five opening
top-line notes of Song 1 (C♯, G♯, F♯, E♯) are replayed in their original
register (in reverse order—F, G♭, A♭, D♭), while A (B♭♭)—the tonic of
Song 1—becomes the bass of an augmented-sixth chord in the key of C♯
(D♭). In the second part, mm. 59ff, there is a final elaborated C♯ (D♭)⁷
chord, (m. 60) followed by a D♯ (E♭) minor triad and other diatonic
harmonies in the key of C♯ (D♭) major. The foreground motivic content
in mm. 61-64 masks linear fourth descents—reversing the fourth ascent
at the start of the postlude—which carry the top line down from G♯ (A♭)
to C♯ (D♭) via the harmonies II-V-I (Ex. 30). The top part then presents

Ex. 30

two direct fourth descents to 5̂ and 3̂, over III and I respectively, before
the closing authentic cadences. The final top-part linear motion, 3̂-2̂-1̂,
parallels the original 5̂-4̂-3̂ (Song 1, mm. 1-2) in an inner part. The final
inner-part motion, a 4̂-3̂ suspension figure, reiterates the opening top-line
connection of Song 1 (Ex. 4), in a context where the C♯ chord is now
entirely consonant in the absence of B♮.

A final word on the correspondence between Songs 12 and 16: the
inclusion of the transposed postlude of Song 12 in the postlude of Song
16 raises the possibility of regarding C♭ (B♮), the tonic of Song 14, as a
large-scale passing-note between B♭, the key of Song 12, and C♯ (D♭),

the key of Song 16. In defense of my view of B♭ as a chromatic passing-note between A (Song 8) and B♮ (Song 14) —cf. pp. 78-79, above—I wish to point out that the correspondence between the two postludes is limited to six measures, after which Song 16 contains another nine bars not previously heard in Song 12. The rationale for the equivalence of the six bars depends upon the internal tonicizations of ♭$\hat{2}$ in each song—C♭ in Song 12, mm. 8-9, and D♮ in Song 16, mm. 48-49. In Song 12, C♭ temporarily reinterprets B♭ as V of E♭ minor; in Song 16, D♮ effects C♯ as V of F♯ minor. The emphasis on the diatonic $\hat{2}$ in the two postludes (as in Ex. 30) reaffirms I in the face of the preceding dominantizing effect of ♭$\hat{2}$. The reaffirmation of B♭ as tonic of Song 12 is just temporary, since B♭ actually becomes V of E♭ minor in Song 13. In Song 16, however, the strong diatonic content of the second part of the postlude dispels the likelihood of regarding C♯ as any scale degree other than I.

A note about performance. I hope that I have demonstrated that the original keys of *Dichterliebe* are essential to the cohesion of the cycle as Schumann conceived of it. True, it may be necessary for singers with low voices to transpose the cycle,[14] but all the songs must be transposed at the same distance if the internal key relationships are to be maintained. Unfortunately, I have found no published edition for low voice where all the songs are transposed at the same interval.[15] The reader stands warned that only performances by tenors—women rarely sing the cycle in public because of its poetic content[16]—can be expected to conform to the original keys. The following is a not necessarily exhaustive list of recordings,[17] arranged alphabetically, in which the correct key relationships are maintained. An asterisk indicates a recording which is presently out of print.

14. It is not completely clear why a singer should wish to perform music that lies outside his range. Violinists generally refrain from performing music composed for the violoncello, etc. See also Schumann's remarks on transposition, p. 132, below.

15. This remark applies even to the Breitkopf & Härtel edition *für mittlere Stimme zum praktischen Gebrauch eingerichtet* made by Clara Schumann (plate number V.A. 608 [188–]) .

16. But Schumann dedicated the cycle to the famous soprano, Schröder-Devrient. Also, note the performances by Lotte Lehmann and Suzanne Danco in the list of acceptable recordings below.

17. The extra four songs are included in a Deutsche Grammophon recording (SLPM 139110) by Dietrich Fischer-Dieskau and Jörg Demus.

*Suzanne Danco, Guido Agosti (London LPS 23)
*Anton Dermota, Hilde Dermota (Telefunken LGX 66023)
*Ernst Haefliger, Eric Werba (Heliodor 25048)
Lotte Lehmann, Bruno Walter (Odyssey 32 16 0315)
*Petre Munteanu, Franz Holetschek (Westminster WN 18010)
Peter Pears, Benjamin Britten (London OSA-1261)
Aksel Schiøtz, Gerald Moore (Danish Odeon MOAK-3)
*Cesare Valetti, Leo Taubman (RCA Victor LM/LSC 2412)
Fritz Wunderlich, Hubert Giesen (Deutsche Grammophon 139125)

The following analyses represent a variety of views concerning Songs 2-5. My purpose in presenting the additional analyses is to offer the reader some alternatives to the analyses presented above, as well as to emphasize the important point that analyses are theories, not facts, and that the presentation of an analysis is never, in and of itself, a disproof of some other analysis of the same work.

The excerpt by Allen Forte uses Schenker's sketches of Song 2 as an illustration of Schenker's analytic theories and techniques, which are the basis for all the analyses presented here.

HEINRICH SCHENKER

[*Song 2*] [†]

The biographical facts of the life of Heinrich Schenker (1867-1935) are hardly commensurate with the importance and influence of his theories in academic circles today. Having, as a young man, caught the attention of Brahms and Busoni, Schenker went on to become a private teacher of piano and theory. He attracted a talented student clientele, some of whom—most notably Oswald Jones, Felix Salzer, and the late Hans Weisse— emigrated to the United States and brought his theories to several universities and conservatories here. Schenker wrote many books and essays, a great number of which were published (in the original German). To date, only his *Harmony* (written in 1906) and *Five Graphic Music Analyses* (dating from his last years) are available in English (along with a few articles). Schenker's culminating work, *Der freie Satz* (Free Composition), was just short of completion at the author's death. Although still available in the original German, no English translation of this important book has yet been published. A survey and discussion of Schenker's basic theoretical ideas can be found in Allen Forte's essay *Schenker's Conception of Musical Structure*[1], a portion of which follows this excerpt.

[†] From *Der freie Satz*, 2nd rev. ed., Anhang, Fig. 22b, p. 8. The commentary appears in the discussion of the concept of "interruption," p. 71 of the main volume. Copyright 1956, Universal Edition; used by permission.

1. *Journal of Music Theory*, III/1 (April, 1959) , 1-30.

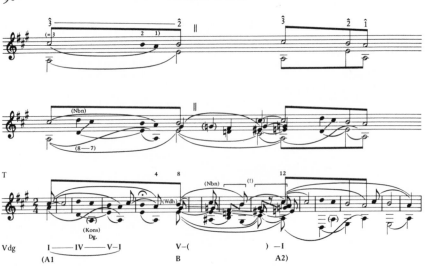

Commentary: The bass carries an arpeggiation of the fifth down through the third without, however, invalidating the interruption.

ALLEN FORTE

[*Schenker's Analysis of Song 2*]†

Allen Forte is one of a handful of American theorists who have been re-
sponsible for promulgating the theories of Schenker in the English-speaking
world. Currently a member of the theory department at Yale University,
Forte is the author of numerous books and articles on theory and for several years was editor of the *Journal of Music Theory*.

I can think of no more satisfactory way to introduce Schenker's ideas,
along with the terminology and visual means which express them, than
to comment at some length upon one of his analytic sketches. For this
purpose I have selected from *Der freie Satz* a sketch of a complete short

† From *Schenker's Conception of Musical Structure*, in *Journal of Music Theory*,
III/1 (April, 1959) , 7-14, 23-24. Reprinted by permission of the *Journal of Music
Theory*, Copyright, 1959.

work, the second song from Schumann's *Dichterliebe* [see above]. I shall undertake to read and interpret this sketch, using, of course, English equivalents for Schenker's terms.[1]

Here in visual form is Schenker's conception of musical structure: the total work is regarded as an interacting composite of three main levels. Each of these structural levels is represented on a separate staff in order that its unique content may be clearly shown. And to show how the three levels interact, Schenker has aligned corresponding elements vertically. I shall make a quick survey of this analytic sketch and then give a more detailed explanation.

The lowest staff contains the major surface events, those elements which are usually most immediately perceptible. Accordingly, Schenker has designated this level as the *foreground*. In deriving his foreground sketch from the fully notated song, Schenker has not included all its actual note values. Those which he does include represent in some cases the actual durational values of the work; but more often they represent the relative structural weight which he has assigned to the particular tone or configuration. This sketch omits repeated tones, and shows inner voices in mm. 8-12[2] only, indicating that there they have greater influence upon the voice-leading.

On the middle staff Schenker has represented the structural events which lie immediately beyond the foreground level. These events, which do not necessarily occur in immediate succession in relation to the foreground, comprise the *middleground*. It should be evident now that the analytic procedure is one of reduction; details which are subordinate with respect to larger patterns are gradually eliminated—in accordance with criteria which I will explain further on.

Finally, on the upper staff, he has represented the fundamental structural level, or *background*, which controls the entire work.

Now let us consider the content of each level in some detail. This will provide an opportunity to examine other important aspects of Schenker's thought, all derived from his central concept.

A series of sketches such as this can be read in several directions.

1. The rendering of Schenker's technical expressions into English presents a number of problems, not the least of which is the fact that there are already, in some cases, two or more published versions of the same term. It is to be hoped that with the publication of *Der freie Satz* (now being translated) a standard nomenclature will be established.

2. The initial *T* which stands at the upper left of the bottom sketch is short for *Takt*, meaning "measure." Measures 5-8 are omitted, as indicated by (*Wdh*) [*Wiederholung*], meaning "repetition". [*Editor*]

For the purpose of the present introductory explanation it would seem advantageous to begin with the level which contains the fewest elements and proceed from there to the level which contains the most—thus, reading from top to bottom or from background to foreground. By reading the sketches in this order we also gain a clear idea of Schenker's concept of *prolongation*: each subsequent level expands, or *prolongs*, the content of the previous level.

The background of this short song, and of all tonal works, whatever their length, is regarded as a temporal projection of the tonic triad. The upper voice projects the triad in the form of a descending linear succession which, in the present case, spans the lower triadic third. Schenker marks this succession, which he called the *Urlinie*, or fundamental line, in two ways: (1) with numerals (and carets) which designate the corresponding diatonic scale degrees, and (2) with the balken [i.e. beam] which connects the stemmed *open* notes (I shall explain the black noteheads shortly). The triad is also projected by the bass, which here outlines the triadic fifth, the tonality-defining interval. Schenker calls this fundamental bass motion *Bassbrechung*, or bass arpeggiation. Like the fundamental line, it is represented in open note-heads. The fundamental line and the bass arpeggiation coordinate, forming a contrapuntal structure, the *Ursatz*, or fundamental structure which constitutes a complete projection of the tonic triad.[3] Thus, to Schenker, motion within tonal space is measured by the triad, not by the diatonic scale.

Observe that in this case the most direct form of the fundamental structure would be the three-interval succession in the outer voices:

fundamental line, $\hat{3}$-$\hat{2}$-$\hat{1}$

bass arpeggiation, I-V-I

The background sketch shows that this succession occurs consecutively only in the last part of the song. The song begins unambiguously with $\hat{3}$: however, it does not progress immediately to $\hat{2}$ and from
I   V

there on to $\hat{1}$; instead, the first interval is *prolonged* as shown in the
I

sketch: the upper voice C♯ first receives an embellishment, or diminution, in the form of the third-spanning motion, C♯–B–A (represented in black noteheads), and then moves over a larger span (shown by the beam) to B on the last eighth-note of m. 8, where it is supported by the bass V. (This

---

3. Each tonal work manifests one of three possible forms of the fundamental line, always a descending diatonic progression: 3-1 (as in the present case), 5-1 and 8-1. Variants upon these forms arise when the bass arpeggiation disposes the fundamental line components in different ways.

V is not to be equated with the final V [m. 15], which effects a closure of the fundamental line.) Schenker then shows how this initial prolongation is followed by a restatement of $\overset{\wedge}{3}$ and the completion of the succession $\underset{I}{\overset{\wedge}{3}\text{-}\overset{\wedge}{2}\text{-}\overset{\wedge}{1}}$ I–V–I.

To recapitulate, there are two prolongational classes shown in this background sketch. The first includes diminutions, or prolongational tones of shorter span (represented by black noteheads) ; the second includes the larger prolongational motion from $\overset{\wedge}{3}$ to $\overset{\wedge}{2}$ (connected by the beam) which comprises the controlling melodic pattern of the first phrase. Schenker regards this larger prolongation motion as an *interruption* of the direct succession, $\underset{\text{I–V–I}}{\overset{\wedge}{3}\text{-}\overset{\wedge}{2}\text{-}\overset{\wedge}{1}}$, and represents it by placing parallel vertical lines above the staff following $\underset{\text{I–V}}{\overset{\wedge}{3}\text{-}\overset{\wedge}{2}}$. The fundamental structure, which is in this case the uninterrupted succession $\underset{\text{I–V–I}}{\overset{\wedge}{3}\text{-}\overset{\wedge}{2}\text{-}\overset{\wedge}{1}}$ therefore may be considered as the essential content of the background.[4] In reading Schenker's analytic sketches a distinction must often be drawn between the background level *in toto*, which sometimes includes prolongations of primary order as in the present case, and the essential *content* of that level, the fundamental structure. Thus, "fundamental structure" designates a specific contrapuntal organization which assumes several possible forms, whereas "background" is a term which may include other events in addition to the fundamental structure, as in the present instance, where it includes two prolongations, each belonging to a different structural order. This distinction, not always clearly drawn by Schenker, is indispensable to the full understanding of his sketches and commentaries. In this connection I point out that within each of the three main structural levels several sub-levels are possible, depending upon the unique characteristics of the particular composition.[5]

The idea of the interrupted fundamental line provides the basis for Schenker's concept of form. For example, in the typical sonata-allegro form in the major mode, interruption of the fundamental linear progression at the close of the exposition normally gives rise in the

4. It should be apparent that Schenker's major concept is not that of the *Ursatz*, as is sometimes maintained, but that of structural levels, a far more inclusive idea.

5. Undoubtedly Schenker compressed many of his sketches in consideration of the practical requirements of publication. Mr. Ernst Oster, who has in his possession a large number of Schenker's unpublished materials—which he plans to present along with commentaries at a future date—has brought this to my attention. Schenker's unpublished sketches of Brahms' *Waltzes*, Opus 39, for example, are executed on several superimposed staves, so that each structural level is shown distinctly and in detail.

development section to a prolongation which centers on V. Of course, the prolonged fundamental line component varies, depending upon which form of the fundamental structure is in operation and upon which specific prolongation motions occur at the background level.

Before explaining the middleground, I should like to direct attention again to the diminution which spans the third below C♯ (black noteheads). By means of the numerals 3, 2, 1, enclosed in parentheses, Schenker indicates that the motion duplicates the large descending third of the fundamental line. This is an instance of a special kind of repetition which Schenker called *Übertragung der Ursatzformen* (transference of the forms of the fundamental structure). Throughout his writings he demonstrates again and again that tonal compositions abound in hidden repetitions of this kind, which he distinguishes from more obvious motivic repetitions at the foreground level.

We can interpret the content of the middleground most efficiently by relating it to the background just examined. The first new structural event shown at the middleground level is the expansion of the smaller prolongational third (black noteheads) by means of the upper adjacent tone,[6] D, which serves as a prefix. The sketch shows how this prolongational element is counterpointed by the bass in such a way as to modify the original (i.e. background) third. That is, the figured-bass numerals in parentheses indicate that the second C♯ (black notehead) is a dissonant passing-tone, and therefore is not to be equated with the initial C♯, which serves as the point of departure for the fundamental line. The adjacent tone D recurs in m. 14, where Schenker assigns more structural weight to it, as indicated by the stem. I reiterate that conventional durational values are used in the analytic sketches to indicate the relative position of a given component or configuration in the tonal hierarchy— the greater the durational value, the closer the element to the background.

In addition to the prolongation described in the preceding paragraph, the middleground contains the essentials of the prolongational middle section (mm. 9-12) which appears in more detail in the foreground sketch. Schenker regards this entire middle section as a prolongation of the background fifth formed by $\frac{5}{V}$. Its main feature is the inner voice which descends from G♯ to E, a middleground duplication of the fundamental line's third. The bass which counterpoints this inner voice arpeggiates the tonic triad, E–C♯–A. Schenker shows how the

6. Schenker's abbreviation, "Nbn," stands for *Nebennote*, or in English, adjacent tone (not "neighbor tone").

arpeggiation is partially filled in by the passing tone, D, and by slurring E to A he indicates that he considers that motion to be the controlling bass motion, within which the C♯ functions as a connective of primarily melodic significance.[7] Here we have an example of the careful distinction which Schenker always draws between major bass components or *Stufen*, which belong to the background level, and more transient, contrapuntal-melodic events at the foreground and middleground levels.

A brief consideration of three additional events will complete our examination of the middleground level. First, observe that the diatonic inner-voice descent in the middle section, G♯–E, is filled in by a chromatic passing-tone, G. Schenker has enclosed this in parentheses to indicate that it belongs to a subsidiary level within the middleground. Second, observe that just before the inner-voice motion is completed on the downbeat of m. 12, the G♯, its point of departure, is restated by an additional voice which is introduced above it. Schenker has pointed out that in "free" compositions, particularly instrumental works, the possibility of more elaborate prolongation is greatly increased by introducing additional voices, as well as by abandoning voices already stated. The final event to observe here occurs in the middle section: the motion from B, the retained upper voice, to C♯ on the downbeat of m. 12. This direct connection does not actually occur at the foreground level, but Schenker, feeling that it is strongly implied by the voice-leading context, encloses the implied C♯ in parentheses and ties it to the actual C♯, thereby indicating that it is an anticipation.

In the foreground sketch Schenker represents for the first time the metrical organization of the song. As I have already mentioned, he shows there some of the actual durational values, in addition to using these as sketch symbols. This reveals the position assigned to meter and rhythm in his system: he considered them to be important structural determinants at the middleground and foreground levels but subsidiary to the fundamental *tonal* organization, which, he maintained, was arhythmic. * * *

Let us now examine some of the relationships which Schenker has shown in his sketch of the foreground, this time beginning with the bass. In m. 3 he encloses the bass-note A in parentheses and marks it with the abbreviation, *Kons. Dg.* (*Konsonanter Durchgang* or "consonant passing-tone"). By this he indicates that the tenth which the bass A forms with

---

7. The author adds here a footnote calling attention to Schenker's remarks, page 96 above, noting that this is one of Schenker's few comments upon this sketch. [*Editor*]

the upper-voice C♯ transforms the latter, a dissonant passing-tone at the middleground level, into a consonance at the foreground level. In this way he also intends to indicate the function of the chord at that point. Since it supports a passing-tone in the upper voice it is a passing chord. In addition, it belongs only to the foreground and therefore is to be distinguished from the initial tonic chord, a background element. Two of Schenker's most important convictions underlie this treatment of detail: (1) that the study of strict counterpoint provides the indispensable basis for a thorough understanding of the details, as well as the larger patterns of a composed work, and (2) that the function of a chord depends upon its context, not upon its label. This can be seen in his notation of the chords in this sketch. Although he uses the conventional Roman numerals he provides them with slurs, dashes and parentheses to show their relative values in the tonal hierarchy. Thus, the long slur from I to I indicates that the IV and V chords lie within the control of that chord, while the abbreviation, *Vdg.* (*Vordergrund*) shows that the succession belongs to the foreground. And in the middle section, mm. 8-12, the parentheses show that the chords between V and I are subsidiary chords. These arise as part of the prolongational complex at that point and stand in contrast to the stable background chords I and V.

Now let us turn to the melody. We can most efficiently examine its structure by first comparing each foreground prolongation (slurred) with the larger middleground prolongation immediately above it, and then by relating both the foreground and middleground to the background. In this way we see that the foreground prolongation of the first section spans a descending third twice, thus duplicating the successively larger thirds at the middleground and background levels. In the middle section the melody undergoes more elaborate development. There, by means of connecting beams, Schenker shows how the upper voice skips down to the inner voice and back again. The ascending skips comprise a sequence of two fourths, which are marked by brackets and emphasized by a typically Schenkerian exclamation point. This sequence lends support to his reading of the implied anticipation of C♯ in the upper voice of m. 12, mentioned earlier.

The foreground of the middle section provides a good example of Schenker's concept of "melody" (he avoided the term in his writings) as a self-contained polyphonic structure. This valuable aspect of his theory,[8]

8. A highly interesting application of this concept is to be found in Schenker's essay, "Das Organische der Fuge" (*Das Meisterwerk in der Musik*, Munich, 1925-30,

which is absolutely indispensable to any kind of intelligent melodic analysis, is well substantiated by compositional practice. There are many passages in the literature where polyphonic melodies, implied at one point (often the beginning) are subsequently realized in full, for example in the first movement of Mozart's *Sonata in A minor*, or in Brahms' *Intermezzo in B♭ major*, Op. 76/4; and, of course, we find a special development of this concept in Bach's compositions for solo violin and for solo cello.[9] Here, in the foreground sketch of the middle section the diagonal beams show that the vocal melody shifts back and forth between two lines, the lower of which belongs to the accompaniment. It is evident that this section contains the most intricate upper-voice prolongation.

It also contains the most elaborate bass motion. The sketch shows how the bass provides counterpoint to the upper-voice (foreground) prolongation of B, bass and upper voice comprising the interval succession 5-10-5-10-5, which is enclosed within the middleground outer-voice succession, $\frac{\text{B—C}\sharp}{\text{E—C}\sharp}$. Observe that the upper voice alternates between an upper adjacent-tone prolongation of B (marked *Nbn.*) and the skips into the inner voice which were explained in the preceding paragraph. The lowest voice in this passage is subordinate to the voice which lies immediately above it, E–D–C♯, the latter succession being the actual bass line (cf. middleground sketch). Nor does its registral position above the foreground bass lessen its importance as the main motion-determinant in the lower voices. Therefore, the foreground bass which displaces or covers it registrally might be termed a "pseudo-bass."[10]

One final aspect of the foreground-sketch deserves mention: the form. Schenker indicates this with the customary letters and exponents. The foreground form therefore corresponds to the form-generating interruption at the middleground and background levels as follows:

Statement	Interruption	Restatement and closure
A[1]	B	A[2]

It should be apparent that an analysis of this kind embraces all the

---

Vol. II), where he employs his technique of synthesis, or reconstruction, to demonstrate that the subject of Bach's *C-minor Fugue* (WTC I) implies a complete, self-contained contrapuntal structure.

9. Cf. Johann David Heinichen, *Der General-Bass in der Composition*, Leipzig, 1728, pp. 558ff: "Das 2-stimmige Harpeggio," "Das 3-stimmige Harpeggio," etc.

10. Relationships of this kind occasionally cause students to be confused; by assigning a structural event to the wrong level they necessarily arrive at a misreading. The technique of reconstruction serves as a corrective in such instances.

information generally included under the heading "form and analysis" but that it goes far beyond to interpret the relationships to the background which are revealed during its initial phases, where the main concern is to achieve an accurate reading of foreground and middleground.

A summary of this analysis should properly include a classification of the chromatic chords in the middle section of the piece, and a more precise explanation of the coordination of linear intervals at the foreground level, the descending thirds and fifths (which latter take the form of diminished fifths and ascending fourths in the middle section). However, because of space limitations, I shall not undertake a summary here, but instead go on to discuss other aspects of Schenker's work. If the preceding commentary has succeeded in demonstrating some of Schenker's more important ideas, as well as clarifying some of the vocabulary and visual devices which he employs to express those ideas, it has fulfilled its purpose.

*   *   *

Schenker approached compositional problems mainly through the principles of strict counterpoint, in the conviction that these underlay the intricate works of the major composers. This belief was supported by his knowledge of the training received by Haydn, Mozart, Beethoven, and others. Nowhere is this fundamental aspect of Schenker's thought more apparent than in the first and third sections of *Der freie Satz*, which comprise a condensed reinterpretation of principles formulated years earlier in *Kontrapunkt*.

With the aid of this methodologically valuable norm, Schenker was able to investigate many aspects of compositional technique which otherwise would have remained inaccessible. Again and again he demonstrated that foreground detail, with its multiple meanings, could be understood only in relation to the middleground and background, which provide definition in accord with the principles of strict counterpoint. As a study technique he occasionally considered alternate solutions in order to reveal compositional determinants more clearly. To illustrate this, I shall undertake to explain the structural factors which determined Schumann's choice of the secondary dominant (A_7) chord in mm. 12-13. * * * (To avoid misunderstanding, I point out that this discussion is not directly related to Schenker's sketch.) In view of the strong tendency of the preceding C♯ major chord to progress to an F♯ minor (VI) chord, the A^7 chord seems abrupt, has the effect of a discontinuous element, and therefore requires special explanation. True, it leads to the upper-voice adjacent tone, D, an essential foreground element which, in accord with the rhythmic pattern already established, as well as with the consistent association of the adjacent-tone motive, D—C♯ with the verbs in the poem, *must* occur on the downbeat of m. 13. But, as shown in

Ex. 1

Ex. 1, the alternate solution, this tone could also be reached without the aid of the A⁷ chord. This indicates that the upper voice did not determine the choice of the A⁷. When the alternate solution (Ex. 1) is considered, the more important function, hence the *raison d'être* of the A⁷, becomes clear. This alternate passage omits the A⁷ but retains the essential features of its immediate context: the preceding C♯ chord and the upper-voice D which follows it. The alternate begins by fulfilling the tendency of the C♯ chord to resolve to F♯ minor. From there it moves through an E chord back to $\overset{\wedge}{3}$ in m. 14.

What features of the original passage are most noticeably missing from the alternate? First, it is apparent that the upper-voice D on m. 14 lacks the support of the IV chord, which was impossible to reach logically beginning from the VI. But the most striking omission in the alternate version is the chromatically descending inner-voice, which, in the original version, begins with the G♯ carried by the C♯ chord, moves through A to G♮ in the A⁷ chord, descends to F♯–F over IV, and finally moves through E to D—C♯ over V⁷I. Observe that this striking inner-voice line concludes in m. 15 with a statement of the characteristic upper-adjacent-tone motive.[10] We can therefore infer that Schumann selected the A⁷ chord in question not only because of its secondary-dominant relation to the IV at m. 14, but primarily because the A⁷ chord carries G♮, an essential component in the long descending line just described. Using Schenker's concept of structural levels as a criterion we can therefore say that the contrapuntal-melodic reason for the A⁷ chord

10. As in mm. 3-4 (7-8) Schumann here requires the accompanist to interlock the hands in such a way that this motive is naturally stressed.

is more important here than the harmonic (fifths relationship) reason. Obviously, expression of the secondary-dominant relationship does not require the presence of the seventh, G; but by "more important" I mean here that G is a component in a configuration which belongs to a higher

Ex. 2

structural level than does the secondary-dominant relationship.[11] In amplification of this, Ex. 2 shows how the inner-voice component A is stated at the beginning of the song, prolonged by the lower adjacent 7 tone, G♯, in the middle section, then in m. 12 begins the descent to C♯. In Schenker's terms, this linear progression is the composing-out of an interval, not a random interval, but in this case the composing-out of the sixth, A–C♯, the inversion of the triadic third which controls the upper-voice motion of the entire song. This third, stated vertically at the very outset of the piece, is also expressed in the bass succession, III-I, a means of associating the outer voices at all levels.

In attempting to ascertain the major compositional determinant in this instance, I do not disregard the influence of the form of the poem and its internal associations. Doubtless Schumann wanted to set the words, *und vor deinem*, which begin the last section, with the same C♯ used at the beginning with the words, *aus meinem*. Also I do not overlook the fact that the chromatic descent of the inner voice in the final measures repeats the inner-voice and bass diminutions of the middle section, an additional means of unification.

11. Here I disagree with Schenker's sketch, which shows the A⁷ chord supporting 3̂. In my opinion 3̂ is supported by the tonic triad in m. 14.

HEINRICH SCHENKER

[Song 3] †

These previously unpublished sketches were made available by Ernst Oster, owner of a large collection of Schenker's unpublished sketches and analyses. The sketches were made in about 1925, and are included in a folder entitled $\hat{3}$, $\hat{5}$, or $\hat{8}$?, which contains several problematic examples regarding the choice of headnote. In Mr. Oster's view, the sketches were neither regarded as a complete analysis, nor intended for publication. Their inclusion here should be of interest mainly to Schenker aficionados.

GLOSSARY

$\hat{8}$ oder $\hat{5}$? raises the question of which scale degree, the octave or fifth, should be regarded as the main initial melodic note (headnote). Subsequent caretted numbers refer to other scale degrees in the melodic descent to 1 at the end of the song.

Slurs, note stems, diagonal lines, etc. generally signify structural relationships among non-adjacent notes in the score. (A few structural markings have been omitted where they appear to duplicate other markings.) However, note-heads and stems may also signify literal durational values, as in the case of eighth-note durational values and barlines throughout sketch [a].

Nbn signifies Nebennote, literally adjacent-note, although more often known as neighbor-note.

Gliederung refers to a structural division. In this case, the melodic descent, $\hat{5}$-$\hat{1}$, is divided by $\hat{3}$, due to the support of that note (F$\sharp$) in the tonic harmony. This is made particularly clear in sketch [c].

Wie übergreifend can perhaps best be rendered as if superimposed. This is a reference to the melodic importance of $\hat{5}$, which takes precedence over the culminating note of the foreground melodic descent, $\hat{2}$.

N.B. Schenker has indicated implied parallel fifths in m. 9, sketch [a]; however, the lower member of the second fifth, B, is not found in the score itself.

† Reprinted by permission of Ernst Oster.

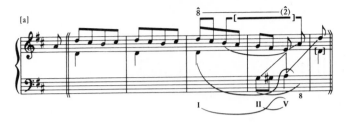

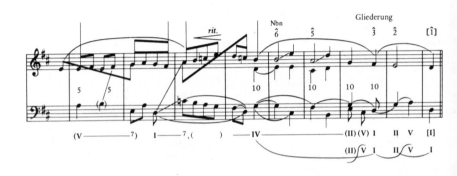

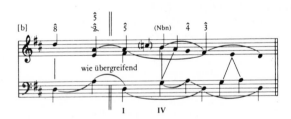

HEINRICH SCHENKER

[*Song 4*]†

FELIX SALZER

[*The Opening of Song 5*]‡

Felix Salzer's *Structural Hearing* (first published in 1952) is the best-known extended treatment of Schenker's ideas in English. Salzer, presently Professor of Music at Queens College of the City University of New York, is co-author of *Counterpoint in Composition* (1969), which is also based on Schenker's teachings. He is the editor of Schenker's *Five Graphic Music Analyses* (2nd ed., 1969), and co-editor of the Schenker-oriented journal *Music Forum*.

---

† From *Der Freie Satz*, 2nd revised edition, *Anhang*, Fig. 152, 1, p. 110. Copyright 1956, Universal Edition, used by permission. The analysis is the first of several with which Schenker illustrates one-part form—cf. p. 200 ff. of the main volume.

‡ From *Structural Hearing*, Dover Publications, New York, 1962, v. 2, Fig. 287, p. 98. The commentary is from volume 1, page 154. Copyright 1952, 1962, Felix Salzer. Reprinted by permission.

Commentary: The impression of introduction is intensified if an incomplete harmonic progression has preceded the structural tonic. . . . This fascinating technique of prolongation creates a certain amount of tension, since the meaning of the prolonging chords is revealed only after the appearance of the I to which the other chords are subordinated. [In this example,] the melodic line B-C♯-D would normally be harmonized by I-V-I (see graph b). However, the support of B with the II⁷ creates an indefinable feeling of tension, so well suited to the inner excitement of the poem (graph a).

COMMENTARY

MENO SPANN

[*The Heine of the Early Poems*][†]

During his student vacations Heine had spent as much time as his uncle[1] would pay for at the newly established North Sea resorts. He loved the sea all his life and it appears with his unhappy love experiences, the joys and sorrows of his student years and even childhood memories in his first large collection of poems *The Book of Songs* published in 1827 when their author was thirty years old. They are the biography of the inner life of Harry—Heinrich Heine. They were also an expression of the *Lebensgefühl* (the way life "felt") prevailing in Germany during the *Biedermeier* period of the restoration. From 1815, when the hope died that revolutionary or military enterprises could redeem suffering Europe, until a similar hope was expressed in the Crystal Palace, that "vitreous expense" which housed the illusion that technology, industry, and the British Empire would be the redeemers, the Germans led the lives of humble subjects and intimidated philistines, At best this age was capable of *holdes Bescheiden* (graceful resignation) as Heine's contemporary, the Swabian poet Mörike, expressed it, but its characteristic way of confronting the adversities of life was sentimental lament.

This sentimental lament prevails in the love poems of the *Book of Songs*, now unbearable to read, though still exquisite as *Lieder* in the settings of Schubert, Schumann, Brahms, Strauss, and other composers. What inspired the composers was the perfect structure, and often elegant antithesis of these ballad-like lyrics, in which unfortunately all of nature with her weeping little flowers and golden little stars and pale roses and saddened larks sympathizes with the unhappy love of the poet whose heart bleeds or breaks whenever rhyme, meter, or climatic effect require it. The best are those in which Heine succeeds in objectivizing the tale

† From Meno Spann, *Heine*, Hillary House Publishers, New York, 1966, pp. 27-33 and 42-43. Reprinted by permission.
1. Salomon Heine, a wealthy banker in Heine's native city, Hamburg. [*Editor*]

of his ruinous love, as in *Lorelei* which has deservedly become a German folksong and with Goethe's *Heidenröslein* the best known German *Lied* in the world. Its fate has a characteristically Heinean irony. During Hitler's tyranny the poem appeared in German song books under "Author unknown"; now it has become a tourist attraction, being played on the Rhine steamers as they pass the Lorelei rock.

As an example, however, of Heine's skill even with a frankly subjective motif (we remember Uncle Salomon's money bags!) let us quote the following poem * * * and note the subtle variation of meaning and intensification of effect achieved in the reiterated refrain:

Du hast Diamanten und Perlen,	Your diamonds and pearls are a treasure
Hast alles, was Menschenbegehr,	What you own is a dream from above
Und hast die schönsten Augen—	Unsurpassed are your eyes in beauty.
Mein Liebchen, was willst du mehr?	My darling, is that not enough?
Auf deine schönen Augen	The praise of your eyes' great beauty
Hab ich ein ganzes Heer	Has so long for me been the stuff
Von ewigen Liedern gedichtet—	For a host of immortal love songs,
Mein Liebchen, was willst du mehr?	My darling, is that not enough?
Mit deinen schönen Augen	Your eyes so radiant so beauteous
Hast du mich gequält so sehr,	Have tortured me, yet it was bluff,
Und hast mich zugrunde gerichtet—	And in the end were my ruin.
Mein Liebchen, was willst du mehr?	My darling, is that not enough?

In other poems the spirit of the *Biedermeier* finds its direct expression. Although Heine rebelled against the sleepy philistines of his age, he was nevertheless sensitive to its tender side, its homely beauty. The following poem presents the charming aspect of the *Biedermeier* in a way we find in the paintings of its artist Spitzweg:

Das ist ein schlechtes Wetter,	That is a wretched weather
Es regnet und stürmt und schneit;	The storm blows rain and sleet,
Ich sitze am Fenster und schaue	I sit at the window gazing
Hinaus in die Dunkelheit.	At the dark, abandoned street.
Da schimmert ein einsames Lichtchen,	There shimmers a light, lone and tiny
Das wandelt langsam fort;	Which slowly moves ahead.
Ein Mütterchen mit dem Laternchen	A little old mother with lantern
Wankt über die Strasse dort.	Comes limping tired and wet.
Ich glaube Mehl und Eier	I think she bought eggs and flour
Und Butter kaufte sie ein;	And butter to make a cake

Sie will einen Kuchen backen Fürs grosse Töchterlein.	For her beloved grown daughter Who lies at home awake.
Die liegt zu Haus im Lehnstuhl Und blinzelt schläfrig ins Licht; Die goldnen Locken wallen Uber das süsse Gesicht.	She lies at home in the arm chair And sleepily blinks into space. Her golden locks move gently Over her sweet young face.

That no false note be heard in the poem from the daughter's being thought lazy, it should be pointed out that she is ill. It was the medical superstition of the age that a rich cake would strengthen the patient.

The complementary aspect of *Biedermeier* appears in this "idyll":

Der bleiche, herbstliche Halbmond Lugt aus den Wolken heraus; Ganz einsam liegt auf dem Kirchhof Das stille Pfarrerhaus.	The pale autumnal halfmoon Peers from a cloudy ledge, In the solitude of the churchyard Lies the old parsonage.
Die Mutter liest in der Bibel, Der Sohn, der starret ins Licht, Schlaftrunken dehnt sich die ältere, Die jüngere Tochter spricht:	The mother reads the bible At the lamplight stares the son The older daughter lolls about Then says the younger one:
'Ach Gott, wie einem die Tage Langweilig hier vergehn! Nur wenn sie einen begraben, Bekommen wir etwas zu sehn.'	'How slowly our days here pass How boring—O my God! The only things we get to see Are burials on this lot.'
Die Mutter spricht zwischen dem Lesen: 'Du irrst, es starben nur vier, Seit man deinen Vater begraben Dort an der Kirchhofstür.'	Still reading says the mother: 'Wrong, there were only eight Since they put to rest your father Next to the churchyard gate.'
Die ältre Tochter gähnet: 'Ich will nicht verhungern bei euch, Ich gehe morgen zum Grafen, Und der ist verliebt und reich.'	The older daughter says yawning: 'I have starved with you enough Tomorrow I will go to the baron Who has money and is in love.'
Der Sohn bricht aus in Lachen: 'Drei Jäger zechen im Stern, Die machen Gold und lehren Mir das Geheimnis gern.'	The son bursts out in laughter: 'Three hunters are drunk in the "Sun". They can make gold and gladly Will teach me how it's done.'
Die Mutter wirft ihm die Bibel Ins magre Gesicht hinein: 'So willst du, Gottverfluchter, Ein Strassenräuber sein!'	The mother throws the bible Into his face so wan 'God's curse upon you, scoundrel Go, be a highwayman!'

Sie hören pochen ans Fenster	They hear a knock at the window
Und sehn eine winkende Hand;	And see a hand point down
Der tote Vater steht draussen	Their own dead father stands outside
Im schwarzen Predgergewand.	In his black preacher's gown.

What could be an idyllic scene is, in this poem, brooding evil born out of boredom. The Bible-reading mother, who is hard of hearing, recognizes all this too late. Her concern for moral respectability has always been great, but she is unable to combat the ennui from which her children suffer and which drives them to seek distraction in questionable adventures. The whole age suffered from that boredom; Büchner, the young rebel and author of *Woyzeck,*[2] expressed it with a curse which came close to what Heine said in his infernal idyll: "Let the fizzled-out modern society go to hell. Its entire life consists of attempts to overcome its frightful boredom." Goethe thanked God "that he was not young in such a thoroughly exhausted world." Rachel,[3] Heine's patroness, called her time "the infinite depth of emptiness."

Most important among Heine's "innovations" is his harsh use of romantic irony so often found in the *Book of Songs* and so often quoted as evidence of insincerity and the sarcasm which supposedly possessed him and made him unfit to be a poet. One example will suffice. In one of his sea poems Heine describes himself lying at an unprotected edge of the ship staring into the water where he sees Vineta, the legendary city, which sank deep into the sea, and at the window in one of the high gabled houses deep down there he discovers his long lost, never forgotten sweetheart who capriciously hid from him, and now cannot return. With outstretched arms the young lawyer wants to throw himself down to join her:

Aber zur rechten Zeit noch	But at the right time still
Ergriff mich beim Fuss der Kapitän,	My foot was seized by the captain.
Und zog mich vom Schiffsrand,	He pulled me to safety
Und rief, ärgerlich lachend:	And shouted angrily laughing:
'Doktor, sind Sie des Teufels?'	'Doctor, what devil rides you?'

Here Heine's so-called cynicism is psychologically the self-defence of the wounded romanticist, as English-speaking critics have been more ready to appreciate.

2. Georg Büchner lived from 1813 to 1837. His psychological drama *Woyzeck* was published posthumously in 1879, and later served as the basis for Alban Berg's famous opera *Wozzeck*, composed in 1925.

3. The wife of Varnhagen von Ense and the hostess of an important cultural salon in Berlin during Heine's sojurn in that city (1821-23).

EDWARD T. CONE

[*Ich grolle nicht*]†

To test this theory [i.e. that a reader of a poem might savor certain words and reread some lines rather than proceed directly from start to finish] I have applied it to one of the extreme examples of the literature: Schumann's version of Heine's *Ich grolle nicht*. Here are the original lyric and Schumann's version, which not only repeats arbitrarily but departs sharply from the correct stanza division:

Heine: Ich grolle nicht, und wenn das Herz auch bricht,
            Ewig verlor'nes Lieb, ich grolle nicht.
            Wie du auch strahlst in Diamantenpracht,
            Es fällt kein Strahl in deines Herzensnacht.

            Das weiss ich längst. Ich sah dich ja im Traum
            Und sah die Nacht in deines Herzens Raum,
            Und sah die Schlang', die dir am Herzen frisst,
            Ich sah, mein Lieb, wie sehr du elend bist.

Schumann: Ich grolle nicht, und wenn das Herz auch bricht,
            Ewig verlor'nes Lieb,
            Ewig verlor'nes Lieb, ich grolle nicht,
                              ich grolle nicht.

            Wie du auch strahlst in Diamantenpracht,
            Es fällt kein Strahl in deines Herzens Nacht,
            Das weiss ich längst.

            Ich grolle nicht, und wenn das Herz auch bricht,
            Ich sah dich ja im Traume,
            Und sah die Nacht in deines Herzens Raume,
            Und sah die Schlang', die dir am Herzen frisst,
            Ich sah, mein Lieb, wie sehr du elend bist.
            Ich grolle nicht,
            Ich grolle nicht.

† From *Words into Music: the Composer's Approach to the Text*, in *Sound and Poetry*, Northrup Frye, ed., New York, 1957, pp. 12-14. Copyright 1957, Columbia University Press. Reprinted by permission.

The repetitions in the first stanza seem to me quite natural and explicable along the lines indicated in the preceding example.[1] The linking of *Das weiss ich längst* with the first stanza is more dubious; yet logically *Das* refers backward rather than forward, and Schumann has certainly made this clear. It is still harder to justify the return to the opening lines immediately afterward, although it is easy to see that Schumann badly needed them for reasons of thematic parallelism. But another motivation was perhaps suggested by Heine himself when he returned to *Ich grolle nicht* at the end of his own second line. These words become, as it were, an *ostinato* motif, heard by implication underneath everything that follows, the purpose of which after all is to explain why the protagonist is not angry even though his heart is breaking. Schumann has made this *ostinato* explicit, and has chosen logical places to do so: after the pause suggested by the connotations of *längst* (a pause lengthened by the musical setting), and at the very end, when the listener's thoughts would naturally return to the initial paradox.

This explanation may not be convincing and I do not insist upon it, but I do insist that it is too facile to claim that every such repetition and rearrangement is an arbitrary violation of the poetic design.

EDVARD GRIEG

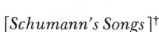

[*Schumann's Songs*]†

In August, 1879, the newly founded *Bayreuther Blätter,* a house organ of the Wagner circle at Bayreuth, published a diatribe on Schumann's music.[1a] The author, Joseph Rubinstein (referred to below by Grieg as "the Bayreuth critic") was a Russian Jew who several years earlier had

1. The reference is to a discussion of Schubert's setting of the *Wanderers Nachtlied* in which repetitions are considered as clear examples of the reader's tendency to pause and linger on certain words of a poem. [*Editor*]

† From Edvard Grieg, *Robert Schumann* in *The Century Magazine,* XLVII (1894), 440-48. The portion quoted may be found on pp. 447-48.

1a. Joseph Rubinstein, *Über die Schumann'sche Musik,* in *Bayreuther Blätter,* II/8, (1879), 216-29.

begged Wagner to take him on as an assistant. This was quite remarkable, inasmuch as Rubinstein (not to be confused with Anton or Nicholas Rubinstein) was fully aware of Wagner's anti-Semitic sentiments—having read his *Das Judenthum in der Musik*—and actually approved of them. Since Rubinstein had both means and talent, Wagner took him on as a rehearsal pianist, and Rubinstein remained a member of the "inner circle" until Wagner's death in 1883. (Rubinstein died a year later by his own hand.) His article on Schumann caused a considerable uproar in the musical world, and, even fifteen years later, Grieg—who had been a student at the Leipzig Conservatory shortly after Schumann's death—felt moved to publish an essay in Schumann's defense.

Intentionally I have chosen to consider last that portion of Schumann's work which proves him to be what, according to his innermost nature, he really was—a poet. I refer to his songs. Even all the demons of hate which possess the Bayreuth critic do not here suffice to reduce the composer to a nonentity. In order to disparage, however, and minimize even this expression of his genius, he resorts to far-fetched humor. I cannot refrain from quoting literally the following choice effusion:

> Since nowadays one does not find it ridiculous when, in our salons, a lady, holding a fan and a fragrant lace handkerchief between her gloved fingers, sings of her former lover as a "lofty star of glory who must not know her, the lowly maid,"[2]—or when a gentleman in swallow-tail coat assures us that he has seen in his dream a serpent feeding on the gloom-engulfed heart of a certain miserable person who shall not be mentioned,[3]—then certainly one ought not, primarily, to be angry with the composer because in his illustration of such poems, popular in our higher circles of society, he has, in his effort not to be outstripped by the poet, sounded all the depths and heights of musical expression.

What a quantity of genuine Wagnerian gall is concentrated in this long-winded monster of a sentence! But—it goes too far. Schumann's songs emerge from this mud-bath as pure as they were before they were dipped into it. If there is anything at all that Schumann has written which has become, and has deserved to become, world literature, it is surely his songs. All civilized nations have made them their own. And there is probably in our own day scarcely a youth interested in music to whom they are not, in one way or another, interwoven with his most intimate ideals. Schumann is the *poet*, contrasting in this respect with

---

2. A line from Schumann's *Frauenliebe und -leben*, Song 2 (*Er, der Herrlichste von allen*). The poem is by Chamisso. [*Editor*]

3. A line from *Dichterliebe*, Song 7 (*Ich grolle nicht*). [*Editor*]

his greatest successor, Brahms, who is primarily *musician*, even in his songs.

With Schumann the poetic conception plays the leading part to such an extent that musical considerations technically important are subordinated, if not entirely neglected. For all that, even those of his songs of which this is true exert the same magic fascination. What I particularly have in mind is his great demand upon the compass of the voice. It is often no easy thing to determine whether the song is intended for a soprano or an alto, for he ranges frequently in the same song from the lowest to the highest register. Several of his most glorious songs begin in the deepest pitch and gradually rise to the highest, so that the same singer can rarely master both. Schumann, to be sure, occasionally tried to obviate this difficulty by adding a melody of lower pitch, which he then indicates by smaller notes placed under the melody of his original conception. But how often he thereby spoils his most beautiful flights, his most inspired climaxes! Two instances among many occur to me— *Ich grolle nicht*, and *Stille Thränen*[4]—for which one will scarcely ever find an interpreter who can do equal justice to the beginning and the end. But if, on the other hand, a singer has a voice at his command capable of such a feat, he will produce the greater effect. Thus, I remember as a child, in 1858, having heard Frau Schröder-Devrient, then fifty-five years old, sing *Ich grolle nicht* and never shall I forget the shiver that ran down my spine at the last climax.[5] The beautiful timbre of the voice was of course lacking; but the overwhelming power of the expression was so irresistible that everyone was carried away.

To be able to sing Schumann is a special faculty which many excellent singers do not have. I have heard the same singer render Schubert to perfection, and Schumann absolutely badly. For with Schubert the most of what is to be done is explicitly expressed; while with Schumann one must understand the art of reading between the lines—of interpreting a half-told tale. A symphony, too, of Schubert plays itself, as it were; but a symphony of Schumann has to be studied with a subtle perception in order to uncover and bring out what is veiled in the master's intentions. Otherwise it will lose much of its effect. In speaking above of the excessive demands upon the compass of the voice in Schumann's songs, I refer chiefly to those more broadly composed. The smaller and

4. Grieg was mistaken in both cases. Only the lower notes are found in the composer's manuscripts of the two songs. The higher optional notes were added later to the published versions. [*Editor*]

5. See footnote 3, p. 119 above. [*Editor*]

more delicate ones do not usually strain a voice of ordinary register.

A quite peculiar stamp of genius is impressed upon Schumann's epic romances and ballads. In this genre he has created unattained masterpieces. I will cite as instances Chamisso's *Die Löwenbraut* and (from Opus 45) Eichendorff's *Der Schatzgräber* and Heine's *Abens am Strand*. In the last named Schumann attains a realistic effect of great intensity. How pictorial is here the description of the different peoples, from the dweller on the banks of the Ganges to the "dirty Laplanders" who in a truly impressionistic style "quack and scream"! Strangely enough, there are as yet not many who both feel and are able to render these effects, and they are accordingly scarcely ever heard in a concert hall. A ballad the popularity of which (according to E. F. Wenzel) [6] vexed Schumann, was Heine's *Two Grenadiers* because he regarded it, and perhaps rightly, as belonging to his weakest productions. A volume which contains things of the very highest order, and which for some incomprehensible reason is almost unknown, is Opus 98[a], *Lieder und Gesänge aus Goethes Wilhelm Meister*. Once in a while one may, to be sure, stumble upon the magnificent, grandly molded ballad, "Was hör' ich draussen vor dem Thor" (*Ballade des Harfners*), but one never hears the most beautiful of all, "Kennst du das Land wo die Zitronen blühn?" with which I have seen a gifted vocalist move an audience to tears.

It is rarely the happiest inspirations of a creative spirit that win the hearts of the many. In that respect the musical intelligence of the so-called cultivated society leaves much to be desired. However, the other arts are scarcely more favorably placed. Everywhere it is cheap art which has a monopoly of appeal to the general intelligence.

It cannot be maintained that Schumann was the first to accord a conspicuous rôle to the accompaniment of his songs. Schubert had anticipated him as no other of his predecessors had done, in making the piano depict the mood. But what Schubert began, Schumann further developed; and woe to the singer who tries to render Schumann without keeping a close watch of what the piano is doing, even to the minutest shades of sound. I have no faith in a renderer of Schumann's songs who lacks appreciation of the fact that the piano has fully as great a claim upon interest and study as the voice of the singer. Nay; I would even venture to assert that, up to a certain point, he who cannot play

6. Ernst Ferdinand Wenzel (1808–80) was Grieg's piano teacher at the Leipzig Conservatory. A friend and colleague of Schumann's, Wenzel contributed articles to Schumann's *Neue Zeitschrift für Musik*, and taught at Leipzig Conservatory from its founding in 1843 until his death. [*Editor*]

Schumann cannot sing him either. In his treatment of the piano, Schumann was furthermore the first who, in a modern spirit, utilized the relation between song and accompaniment, which Wagner has later developed to a degree that fully proves what importance he attached to it. I refer to the carrying of the melody by the piano, or the orchestra, while the voice is engaged in the recitative. Heaven preserve me, however, from insinuating that Wagner consciously could have received an impulse from Schumann! A dyed-in-the-wool Wagnerian would, of course, regard even a hint of such a possibility as an outrageous want of respect for the master of Bayreuth which would amount almost to an insult. But, for all that, it is a fact that contemporaries influence each other whether they want to or not. That is one of nature's eternal laws, to which we are all subject. You will perhaps ask where is, then, the mutual influence of Rossini, Beethoven, and Weber? And my response is: it is of a negative character, and accordingly still present. But in the above-mentioned particular case—that of Schumann and Wagner—it is absolutely positive. It is, however, true that Schumann only hints at things out of which Wagner constructs a perfect system. But there is this to be said, that Schumann is here the foreseeing spirit who planted the tree which later, in the modern musical drama, was to bear such glorious fruit.

LEON B. PLANTINGA

[*Schumann's Conversion to Vocal Music*]†

Though Schumann never said so, he must have included himself among the younger set of composers who cultivated the new, potently expressive style of lied. Three years before he wrote the Franz review[1] Schumann

† From *Schumann as Critic*, New Haven, Yale University Press, 1967, pp. 179-83. Copyright © 1967 by Yale University. Reprinted by permission. In the footnotes, *Briefe* refers to *Robert Schumann's Briefe, Neue Folge*, F. Gustav Jansen ed., Leipzig, 1904, and *NZfM* refers to Schumann's journal, *Neue Zeitschrift für Musik*.

1. In 1843, on the occasion of reviewing Robert Franz's first set of lieder, Schumann described the modern trend in lied composition; cf. p. 129 below. [*Editor*]

took a step that has always puzzled and intrigued students of nineteenth-century music. In 1840, after compiling twenty-three opus numbers of piano music alone,[2] Schumann abruptly shifted to lieder composition; in that year and the following one he turned out a prodigious number of them—the Heine cycle, *Myrthen*, the *Frauenliebe und -leben*, the *Dichterliebe*, and many others. Of his entire output of lieder, in fact, more than half were composed in 1840 alone. And, as we have seen, it was precisely at this time that Schumann the critic, too, began to show a really lively interest in lieder.

Instead of looking for the causes of this sudden change of direction, it might seem more appropriate to inquire why it did not happen earlier. Schumann's love of poetry, the easy blending of his musical and literary talents in his early writings, as well as his unshakable belief in the closeness of literature and music—stated and elaborated upon as early as 1828—would surely lead one to expect from him an earlier interest in the lied.

To find satisfactory answers to the question about Schumann's *Liederjahr*, to understand, in fact, the whole course of Schumann's musical development, it is essential to understand first his profound attachment to that romantic musical instrument par excellence, the piano. All his early musical experiences had been at the keyboard. The music that elicited the immoderate Jean-Paulian effusions of the early diaries and letters was almost always piano music, and his own musical response to the stimulus of romantic literature took the form of improvisations at the piano. Schumann returned to Leipzig from Heidelberg in 1831 with but one purpose: to fulfill a burning ambition to become a piano virtuoso. The musicians with whom he associated in Leipzig were almost all pianists, including the three with whom he collaborated to found the NZfM—a journal devoted to improving conditions in piano music. So strong an attachment to his instrument was not easily broken; Schumann's musical thinking was so solidly rooted in the piano that any rapprochement in his composition between music and literature was almost bound to take the form, not of vocal composition, but, as it did, of programmatic music for piano.

Many reasons have been suggested for Schumann's sudden plunge, finally in 1840, into vocal music: emotional stresses attendant to his

---

2. Schumann had privately tried his hand at lieder, we have seen, as early as 1828 when he set some verses of Kerner and sent them to the composer Gottlob Wiedebein for criticism. See *Briefe*, pp. 6-7.

difficulties with Wieck and impending marriage to Clara, a decline in his imagination, a wish for more "definite expression," and others.[3] While some of these explanations are plausible enough, Schumann's own writings, read attentively, provide more compelling ones. His turn to vocal music in the early 1840s is part of a larger pattern—it is a symptom of his shifting ideas about the progress of romantic music and the future of German musical traditions. That Schumann thought about such expansive questions specifically in connection with lieder is quite clear from the Franz review.

During his earlier years as a critic, too, Schumann was always preoccupied with piano music; all problems of musical style were reduced in his mind to problems about piano music and piano playing. Composers were heroes or villains depending upon what they did or did not do at the piano. Most of the contemporary composers whose music interested Schumann, especially before 1840, concentrated on short pieces for piano—as did, of course, Schumann himself. While Schumann showed a lively interest in this music, reviewing in the 1830s literally hundreds of etudes, capriccios, rondos, and the like, he viewed these pieces only as a kind of preparatory study for the more important business of writing sonatas, concertos, and symphonies. A familiar refrain in Schumann's criticism is his warning against a prolonged preoccupation with these small forms. In a review of assorted short pieces for piano by J. C. Kessler in the first volume of the NZfM, Schumann says he hopes this young composer will soon stop "dissipating" his talents in such music.[4] In 1837 Schumann frets that Chopin always writes short genre pieces instead of the larger forms (part of the trouble, Schumann speculates, is that Chopin is living in Paris.)[5] Not long after, he advises Henselt, in a review of his Etudes Op. 5, to discontinue his efforts along these lines and write in the "higher forms: the sonata or concerto."[6] Schumann repeatedly gave the same advice to Heller[7] and Bennett.[8]

Schumann long took for granted that the real future for the romantic movement, founded by Beethoven, lay in the cultivation of Beethoven's kind of music: the large instrumental forms. But writing sonatas and

3. See F. Feldmann, *Zur Frage des 'Liederjahres' bei Robert Schumann*, in *Archiv für Musikwissenschaft*, 9 (1952), 246.

4. NZfM, *1* (1834), 114.

5. NZfM, *7* (1837), 200.

6. NZfM, *10* (1839), 74.

7. NZfM, *14* (1841), 181-82; *18* (1843), 13.

8. NZfM, *17* (1842), 175; *19* (1843), 17.

symphonies, as he well knew, often simply was not possible early in a composer's career. An enriched harmonic idiom, original rhythms and textures—all the elements of the heightened expressiveness he valued— could best be explored by a young composer, he conceded, in short piano pieces. But he expected the most promising composers of his generation to do as he himself hoped to do: to get about the really important business, sooner or later, of producing extensive instrumental works in a modern style.

In about 1839 Schumann began to show signs of doubt that this would ever happen. In April of that year he observed that most of the sonata composers were neither the romantics nor the composers left over from the preceding generation, but young unknowns for whom the category was nothing but an exercise in form.[9] In July he remarked sadly on the backwardness of the few contemporary symphonies—almost all of them imitated the early style of Beethoven, or even that of Haydn and Mozart. Schumann mentioned one conspicuous exception—the *Symphonie fantastique* of Berlioz.[10] But it is perfectly clear that by this time Berlioz' orchestral works hardly exemplified what Schumann had in mind for a continuation of the romantic tradition of Beethoven and Schubert. Already in June of 1838 Schumann saw that the string quartet, too, was not a very live category; the only really competent composers writing quartets were Mendelssohn and Onslow.[11] Two months later Schumann was excited by the quartets he reviewed in manuscript of an unknown young composer, Herrmann Hirschbach.[12] But Hirschbach apparently produced nothing more, and by the time his quartets were published in 1842, Schumann's enthusiasm for them had cooled.[13]

Schumann began to see at the end of the 1830s that instrumental music was not progressing, and was not likely to progress as he had hoped. The traditional large forms of instrumental music were in danger of extinction, and the romantic composers did not seem particularly interested in reviving them. Schumann himself had serious difficulties in constructing large movements, and at the same time he thought little was to be gained in a continued preoccupation with short pieces for piano. By 1840 instrumental music had in Schumann's opinion arrived at a kind of impasse. A change of direction in his interests was only

9. NZfM, *10* (1839) , 134.
10. NZfM, *11* (1839) , 1.
11. NZfM, *8* (1838) , 194.
12. NZfM, *9* (1838), 51.
13. See NZfM, *16* (1842) , 159.

natural; in his careers both as composer and critic he abruptly turned to vocal music.

There was another factor operative in Schumann the critic's shift of interest. The NZfM had been founded largely to assail the Parisian virtuosi's tyrannical rule over piano music, and Schumann's early criticism was firmly committed to this cause. But by the end of the 1830s this battle was drawing to a close; the greatest vogue of the virtuosi was fading, and the romantic composers were more and more given a hearing. In the Franz review, Schumann describes this struggle against the *Floskel-wesen* [showy mannerisms] in piano music very much in retrospect; it was clearly over, he felt, and the initial goals of his own work as a critic had been achieved. Thus Schumann's feeling about instrumental music in 1840 was strangely divided. He saw a victory being won against Philistinism and gross vulgarization; but this victory was a hollow one in the face of growing doubts, amounting at times to disillusionment, about the direction instrumental music was now to take. Both parts of this dichotomy are mentioned in the Franz review. "The passage-work pieces," Schumann says, "gave way to more thoughtful structures in which one could detect the influence of two masters in particular: Beethoven and Bach." But he says, too, somewhat despondently, "And in truth, the lied is the only category, perhaps, in which there has been really significant progress since Beethoven."[14]

For anyone wishing to explain Schumann's conversion to vocal music in 1840, a bothersome obstacle is raised by his statement in a letter to Herrmann Hirschbach of June 1839: "all my life I have considered vocal composition inferior to instrumental music—I have never regarded it as a great art. But don't tell anyone about it!"[15] What is surprising about this statement is when Schumann said it. By the middle of 1839, shortly before he was to plunge into almost exclusive composition of lieder, his earlier ideas about the relative importance of instrumental and vocal music must surely have been changing—and his use of the present perfect tense (which in German often refers to completed actions) may reflect this. But even if the statement is taken as his current opinion, it is important to notice to whom the letter is addressed. Hirschbach was a contributor to the NZfM whose impatience with the present state of affairs in music and whose impetuous way of expressing himself were reminiscent of the early days of the journal. And shortly before, Schumann had first seen Hirschbach's quarters—music that had

14. NZfM, *19* (1843), 35.
15. *Briefe*, p. 158.

temporarily kindled in him a new excitement and optimism about the future of instrumental music.[16] Hirschbach's writing and music revived in Schumann a spark of his earlier sanguine expectations, and for a moment pushed aside his uncertainty about what an instrumental composer can possibly do after Beethoven. The letter to Hirschbach must be seen in this context.

ROBERT SCHUMANN

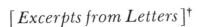

[*Excerpts from Letters*][†]

To Pastor Keferstein, February 2, 1840 (Jansen, No. 191)

I can scarcely tell you what a pleasure it is to write for the voice compared to instrumental composition—and how this rages and surges within me when I sit down to work.

To Clara Wieck, February 22, 1840 (*Jugendbriefe*, p. 309)

Do not be annoyed if today I do not write you much. Since early yesterday I have put down 27 pages of music—something new [*Myrthen*, Op. 25]—about which I can say nothing more than that I laughed and cried for joy.

To Clara Wieck, May 15, 1840 (*Jugendbriefe*, p. 314)

I have again composed so much that sometimes it makes me quite uneasy. But I cannot do anything else—I'd like to sing myself to death like a nightingale. There are twelve Eichendorff songs [*Liederkreis*, Op. 39]. These are already forgotten and something new started.

To Clara Wieck, May 31, 1840 (*Jugendbriefe*, p. 314)

I can't wait for you to come, and for you to tear me away from my music. You will be amazed at how much is finished in this short time and awaits copying. Now I should at last stop, but I cannot. . . .

16. See *Briefe*, pp. 156 and 158, and NZfM, *9* (1838), 42, and 51-52.
† For the purpose of identifying the source of each excerpt, "Jansen" refers to *Robert Schumanns Briefe, Neue Folge,* F. Gustav Jansen, ed., Leipzig, 1904, and *Jugendbriefe* refers to *Jugendbriefe von Robert Schumann,* Clara Schumann, ed., Leipzig, 1895. Translations are by the present editor.

I have now completed Op. 22. I never would have thought it when I wrote Op. 1—in eight years 22 works are quite enough; now I shall do twice as much and then die. . . . Sometimes it seems to me as if I were striking a new way in music.[1]

To Carl Kossmaly, May 9, 1841 (Jansen, No. 223)

I was a little disappointed that in your article[2] you put me in the second class. I did not expect to be put in the first class; but I believe that I have a claim to an individual place, and am hardly pleased to see myself grouped with Reissiger, Curschmann, etc. I know that my aspirations and abilities far exceed theirs, and I hope that you yourself will appreciate this and not think me conceited, which is really not the case. I write this to you candidly and sincerely; I hope you will take it this way. . . .

To A. Kahlert, May 10, 1842 (Jansen, No. 237)

I wish you would get to know my songs better. They foretell my future. I dare not promise more than I have already achieved (in the lieder) , and I am quite satisfied with what I have done so far.

---

1. Schumann was in the process of completing *Dichterliebe* when he wrote this letter. The reference to twenty-two works is puzzling, since by the middle of 1840 he had composed twenty-three piano works, as well as several song cycles. [*Editor*]

2. Kossmaly (1812-93) contributed a series of articles on the state of the lied for Schumann's *Neue Zeitschrift für Musik*. In one of the articles, Vol. 14, No. 16 (February 22, 1841), Kossmaly listed three categories of lied composers, the first being trivial, the second good, and the third the finest. Apparently, Kossmaly included Schumann in the second category, but—in his role as editor—Schumann modestly [*sic*] omitted his name from the article. In the letter, Schumann inadvertently refers to the first category as if it were the best of the three. [*Editor*]

ROBERT SCHUMANN

[*Excerpts from Articles*]†

"I shall not set forth what a beautiful song is," Schumann remarks in a review written in 1840,[1] but in fact he did say a great deal about his attitude toward songs and song composition in his role as editor and reviewer of the *Neue Zeitschrift für Musik*, which he founded in 1834.

CONTEMPORARY DEVELOPMENTS IN LIED COMPOSITION

[THEODOR KIRCHNER (1823-1903), *Zehn Lieder für eine Singstimme mit Pianoforte,* Op. 1 (II, 123)] Along with the progress in the art of poetry, the epoch of Franz Schubert has now been followed by a new one, which is notable for the exploitation of the continually improving accompanying instrument, the piano. The composer calls his songs "Lieder with Pianoforte," and this is not to be overlooked. The voice part alone can in any case not do everything—cannot reproduce everything; aside from the overall feeling, the finer details of the poem should stand out, providing that the melody does not suffer as a result. But this is just what this young composer needs to pay attention to. His songs often seem like independent instrumental pieces which hardly need the voice in order to achieve a complete effect; they are often merely like translations of the poems for the piano—songs without words, in fact, but inspired by words; the melody in them appears often like a mild hint of the words, and the primary content lies mostly in the accompaniment . . .

[ROBERT FRANZ (1815-92), *12 Gesänge* (II, 147)] About the songs of R. Franz there is much to say; they are not a unique phenomenon but

† From Robert Schumann, *Gesammelte Schriften über Musik und Musiker,* Martin Kreisig, ed., 5th ed., 2 vols., Leipzig, 1914. The works under review, and the respective volume and page numbers are given in brackets at the beginning of each excerpt. Translations are by the present editor.

1. "Auseinandersetzen, was ein schönes Lied, will ich nicht." *Ibid,* I, 494.

fit in rather with the whole development of our art in the last ten years. We know that in the years 1830-34 a reaction set in against the prevailing values. The fight was not basically a hard one; it was against the showy mannerisms which—with the exception of a few composers such as Weber, Loewe, etc.—were to be found in all types of music, particularly piano music. . . . Franz Schubert had prepared the way for the [improvement in the] lied, but mainly in the Beethoven manner . . . To hasten the development, there was a new school of German poets: Rückert and Eichendorff . . . Uhland and Heine. . . . Thus, there arose that deeper, more artistic kind of lied which naturally was not known to the earlier composers, since it was the new poetic spirit which was being reflected in the [new] music. The songs of R. Franz belong to this new and noble category. The wholesale fabrication of lieder, which takes as much pleasure in setting jingles as a poem of Rückert, begins now to be recognized for what it is; and if the general public is still not aware of this change, it has been long since made clear to those in the know. And in reality, the lied is perhaps the only type of music in which meaningful progress has been made since Beethoven.

ACCOMPANIMENTS

[NORBERT BURGMÜLLER (1810-36), *6 Gesänge*, Op. 6 (I, 432)] The retention of a single figuration throughout an entire song was something new that was introduced by Franz Schubert; young composers are warned lest this becomes a mannerism.

[HUBERT FERDINAND KUFFERATH (1818-96), *6 Lieder* (II, 83)] We observe in nearly all of these songs the peculiarity of an accompaniment that almost continually moves with the voice, so that the piano part of each song can be played independently of the voice part. This is not a good trait in a song, and it hampers the singer considerably; but we encounter the same thing in all those young composers who have preferred to occupy themselves with instrumental composition[2] . . .

[CARL FRIEDRICH ZÖLLNER (1800-60), *9 Lieder* (II, 84)] The simplicity [of Zöllner's songs] has to do specifically with the accompaniment, which—just the reverse of the songs of Kufferath described above—are

2. In view of Schumann's own background as a composer who initially wrote almost exclusively for the piano, this remark—coming in 1843, three years after his own conversion to lieder—can only appear to be ironic. Schumann died just two years before Wasielewski's full-scale biography appeared in 1858, containing a strenuous castigation of Schumann's ability as a lied composer. Wasielewski's main objection was that Schumann had no understanding of the voice, treating it too much like an instrument by making excessive demands on a singer's vocal range. [*Editor*]

weak and virtually meaningless without the voice part. In Zöllner's songs, the melody in the voice part is the main thing; in order to do justice to their spiritual depth a singer must understand how to recite, and just as the songs follow every nuance of the poems, so we need a singer who is highly sensitive to these [nuances]. How often are we fortunate enough to encounter this? Good lieder singers are almost as rare as good lieder composers . . .

THE QUALITY OF THE TEXT

[WENZEL HEINRICH VEIT (1806-64), *6 Gesänge* (I, 495)] It satisfies him to set poems of slight value . . . talent does not desert [him] in setting such slight poems, but certainly it will blossom into a richer and fresher talent when he picks better poets, like Heine and Mosen . . .

[FRANZ SCHUBERT (1797-1828) (I, 327)] Not much over thirty when he died, he wrote an astonishing amount . . . His songs have spread the fastest and furthest; he would have eventually set the whole of German literature to music, and Telemann, who insisted that a proper composer should be able to set a public notice [*Torzettel*] to music, would have found his man in Schubert. Wherever he reached, music gushed forth: Aeschylus and Klopstock, so reticent to be set to music, gave in to his hands, just as he drew forth the deepest qualities from the facile style of W. Müller and others.

DECLAMATION

[BURGMÜLLER, *5 Gesänge*, Op. 10 (I, 495)] I would prefer that the melody of the earlier verse were not repeated, and that a new one had been composed, especially as in what precedes there are several small errors in declamation which call for censure.

[VEIT, *6 Gesänge* (I, 495)] There is no lack of fine little details in the accompaniment, but truly there is no shortage of little errors in declamation either—slight enough for us to overlook in students, but big enough when made by an imaginative talent for us to gently call attention to them.

INTERPRETATION OF POETRY

[BURGMÜLLER, Op. 6 (I, 432)] We find everything here that we may expect from a song: comprehension of the poetry, fine detail, a happy relationship between voice and piano, an overall selectivity, insight, and warmth.

[JOSEPH KLEIN (1801-62), *6 Gedichte aus Wilhelm Meister von Goethe* (I, 272)] It seems to me that the composer was afraid that he might injure his poem if he took hold of it too hard . . . The poem should be for the singer like a bride in one's arms—free, happy, complete.

[BURGMÜLLER, Op. 10 (I, 495)] The song is one of the best of the collection, . . . But that call "from above" sounds too slack to me. I think that angels call out in a different way; but actually who has ever heard such voices? Whoever on occasion has, had best keep still about it!

[KLEIN, *Der Wirthin Töchterlein* (Uhland) (I, 273)] The idea of starting the song with *Gaudeamus igitur* would be a good one, if it were not that the declamation of the words gets in the way here and there. The first half of the innkeeper's wife's reply suits me altogether, but the second half seems to me unsuitable. Genuine misery does not sound like that, even among the lower classes.

[BERNHARD KLEIN (1793-1832), *3 Gesänge von Goethe* (I, 270)] In the last group of Goethe songs, the second and especially the third strike me as excellent; however, in the Mignon song, *Kennst du das Land*, I miss the grace, if not the pained sentiment, with which the words confront us, as from a heavenly face.

[J. KLEIN, *6 Gedichte* (I, 272)] It pains me that in *Kennst du das Land*, the expressive *dahin* [literally 'thither' (Ed.)] is treated so lightly by most composers, as a sixteenth note[3] . . . It should be treated with more sentiment and greater accent, as one finds in most of the well-known composers. What is still worse is that not one of these settings, with the exception of Beethoven's, approaches in the slightest the effect the poem makes by itself without the music.[4]

TRANSPOSITION

(I, 105). It is certain that the transposition of a composition from the original key into another will produce a different effect, and that

3. Presumably Schumann meant that the first syllable (*da-*) lasts for just a sixteenth note. In Beethoven's setting of the poem, *da* is presented four times as an eighth note in 6/8 meter in a relatively fast tempo, then twice more in melismas lasting half a bar each. Schubert repeats *dahin* many times, the *da* lasting an eighth note in all cases except for one occurrence as a quarter note. In his own setting of the poem (composed in 1849 and found both as Op. 79/29 and Op. 98a/1), Schumann gives *da* an eighth note, forte, in slow tempo. Presumably the treatment of *da* that Schumann would have admired most is Hugo Wolf's, dating from some thirty-two years after Schumann's death. In this setting, the *da* lasts for three eighth notes, and occurs syncopated, during the first beat of the bar, rather than as an upbeat. [*Editor*]

4. It is not clear whether Schumann meant to include Schubert, whom he generally admired, among the composers whose settings fall short of the poem taken by itself. [*Editor*]

there is a pronounced difference in the character of the keys. If, for example, you play the *Desire Waltz* in A major[5] or the *Bridal Chorus* in B major[6], the new keys will have an adverse feeling, because the general mood which every piece generates will appear to be maintained in foreign surroundings. The process by which the composer chooses this or that key for the expression of his feelings is as unclear as the achievement of genius itself . . . The composer finds the right [keys] in much the same way that the painter selects [the right] colors.

5. A composite drawn from Schubert's *Trauenwalzer* and Himmel's *Favorite-Walzer*. The original key is A♭ major. [*Editor*]

6. *Chor der Brautjungfern* from Carl Maria von Weber's opera *Der Freischütz.* The original key is C major. [*Editor*]

Bibliography

WRITINGS BY AND ABOUT SCHUMANN

Schumann, Robert, *Briefe: Neue Folge*, 2nd ed., F. Gustav Jansen, ed., Leipzig, 1904; English version: *The Life of Robert Schumann told in his Letters*, transl. by May Herbert, London, 1890.

Schumann, Robert, *Gesammelte Schriften über Musik und Musiker*, Leipzig, 1854; 5th ed., Martin Kreisig, ed., 2 vols., Leipzig, 1914; English version: *Music and Musicians*, 2 vols., Fanny Ritter, ed. and transl., London, 1877-80.

Schumann, Robert, *Jugendbriefe*, Clara Schumann, ed., Leipzig, 1886.

Schumann, Robert, *Letters*, Karl Storck, ed., transl. by Hannah Bryant, London, 1907.

Schumann, Robert, *On Music and Musicians* [selected writings], Konrad Wolff, ed., transl. by Paul Rosenfeld, New York, 1946; paperback, 1969.

Schumann, Robert, *The Musical World of Robert Schumann* [selected writings], Henry Pleasants, ed. and transl., New York, 1965.

Abert, Hermann, *Robert Schumann*, 4th ed., Berlin, 1920. Ch. 8, *Das Lied*, pp. 78-86, includes a detailed discussion of *Dichterliebe*.

Abraham, Gerald, *Schumann*, in *Grove's Dictionary of Music and Musicians*, 5th ed., London, 1954, VII, 603-40.

Abraham, Gerald, ed., *Schumann, A Symposium*, London, 1952.

Eismann, Georg, *Robert Schumann, Ein Quellenbuch über sein Leben und Schaffen*, 2 vols., Leipzig, 1956.

Fuller-Maitland, J. A., *Robert Schumann*, London, 1884.

Grieg, Edvard, *Robert Schumann*, in *The Century Magazine*, XLVII (1894), 440-48.

Lippman, Edward A., *Schumann*, in *Die Musik in Geschichte und Gegenwart*, Kassel, 1965, XII, 271-326.

Liszt, Franz, *Schumann (1855)*, in *Gesammelte Schriften*, IV, 1880-3; English transl. in *Musical Times*, XCVII (July, 1956), 317 ff.

Plantinga, Leon B., *Schumann As Critic*, New Haven, 1967.

Reissman, August, *The Life and Works of Robert Schumann*, transl. by Abby L. Alger, London, 1886.

Rubinstein, Joseph, *Über die Schumann'sche Musik*, in *Bayreuther Blätter*, II/8 (1879), 216-29.

Schauffler, Robert Haven, *Florestan: The Life and Work of Robert Schumann*, New York, 1945.

Schnapp, Friedrich, *Heinrich Heine und Robert Schumann*, Hamburg, 1924; English transl. by Theodore Baker in *The Musical Quarterly*, XI (1925), 599-616.

Spitta, Philipp, *Schumann*, in *Grove's Dictionary of Music and Musicians*, 1st ed., London, 1883, III, 384-421.

Wasielewski, W. J. von, *Robert Schumann* (1858), 4th ed., Leipzig, 1906; English transl. by Abby L. Alger, Boston, 1871.

WRITINGS BY AND ABOUT HEINE

Heine, Heinrich, *Werke*, 7 vols., Ernst Elster, ed., Leipzig and Vienna, 1890. (*Lyrisches Intermezzo* in I, 63-92.)

Heine, Heinrich, *Lyric Intermezzo*, in *Heine's Book of Songs*, transl. by John Todhunter, Oxford, 1907.

Arnold, Matthew, *Heinrich Heine*, in *Essays in Criticism* (1865), New York, 1930, pp. 156-93.

Atkins, H. G., *Heine*, London, 1929.

Closs, A., *The Genius of the German Lyric*, rev. ed., New York, 1962.

Eliot, George, *German Wit: Heinrich Heine* (1856), in *The Essays of George Eliot*, Thomas Pinney, ed., New York, 1963, pp. 216-54.

Fairley, Barker, *Heinrich Heine, an Interpretation*, Oxford, 1954.

Müller, Günther, *Geschichte des deutschen Lieder*, Munich, 1925.

Mustard, Helen Meredith, *The Lyric Cycle in German Literature*, New York, 1946.

Prawer, S. S., *Heine: Buch der Lieder*, New York, 1962.

Rose, William, *The Early Love Poetry of Heinrich Heine, an Inquiry into Poetic Inspiration*, Oxford, 1962.

Spann, Meno, *Heine*, New York, 1966.

Stein, Jack M., *Schubert's Heine Songs*, in *Journal of Aesthetics and Art Criticism*, XXIV/4 (Summer 1966), 559-66.

Walzel, Oskar, *Deutsche Romantik*, 5th ed., 1923; English version: *German Romanticism*, transl. by Alma Elise Luissky, New York, 1932.

GENERAL LITERATURE ABOUT THE LIED

Bischoff, Hermann, *Das deutsche Lied*, Leipzig, 1905. Specifically on Schumann, pp. 48 ff.

Bücken, Ernst, *Das deutsche Lied*, Hamburg, 1939.

Earl, Don Lee, *The Solo Song Cycle in Germany* 1800-1850, unpublished Ph.D. diss., University of Indiana, 1952.

Elson, Louis C., *German Song*, Boston, 1888. Chs. 20 and 21 on Schumann, pp. 166-87.

Hall, James Husst, *The Art Song*, Norman, Oklahoma, 1953.

Jolizza, W. K. von, *Das Lied und seine Geschichte*, Vienna, 1910.

Miller, Philip L., *The Art Song*, in *The Ring of Words*, New York, 1963, pp. xiii-xx.

Moser, Hans Joachim, *Das deutsche Lied seit Mozart*, 2 vols., Berlin and Zurich, 1937.

Prawer, S. S., *Introduction*, in *The Penguin Book of Lieder*, Baltimore, 1964, pp. 11-17.

Radcliffe, Philip, *Germany and Austria*, in *A History of Song*, Denis Stevens, ed., New York, 1961, pp. 228-64.

Stein, Jack M., *Was Goethe Wrong about the Nineteenth-Century Lied? An Examination of the Relation of Poem and Music*, in *Publications of the Modern Language Association*, LXXVII/3 (June 1962), 232-39.

WRITINGS ABOUT SCHUMANN'S SONGS

Cooper, Martin, *The Songs*, in *Schumann: A Symposium*, Gerald Abraham, ed., London, 1952, pp. 98-137.

Duval, R., *'L'Amour du Poète' de Schumann-Heine*, in *Rivista Musicale Italiana*, VIII (1901), 656-73.

Felber, Rudolph, *Schumann's Place in German Song*, in *The Musical Quarterly*, XXVI (1940), 340-54.

Gadski, Johanna, *The Song Masterpieces of Robert Schumann*, in *Etude*, XXVIII/6 (1910), 371; XXVIII/7 (1910), 449.

Hull, A. Eaglefield, *On A Song-cycle of Schumann [Dichterliebe]*, in *Monthly Musical Record*, LIV (Nov. 1924), 321-23.

Walker, Ernest, *The Songs of Schumann and Brahms—Some Contacts and Contrasts*, in *Music and Letters*, III (1922), 9-19.

Wolff, Victor Ernst, *Robert Schumanns Lieder in ersten und späteren Fassungen*, Leipzig, 1914.

WRITINGS ABOUT THE
ROMANTIC PERIOD

Abraham, Gerald, *A Hundred Years of Music*, 3rd ed., Chicago, 1964.

Ambros, A. W., *Die Neu-romantische Musik*, Leipzig, 1860.

Barzun, Jacques, *Berlioz and the Romantic Century*, 3rd ed., New York, 1969.

Dannreuther, Edward, *The Romantic Period (The Oxford History of Music*, Vol. 6) 2nd ed., London, 1931.

Einstein, Alfred, *Music in the Romantic Era*, New York, 1947.

Hadow, W. H., *Robert Schumann and the Romantic Movement in Germany*, in *Studies in Modern Music*, 1st series, London, 189?.

Leichtentritt, Hugo, *Music, History and Ideas*, Cambridge, 1940.

Ninck, Martin, *Schumann und die Romantik in der Musik*, Heidelberg, 1929.